Choicez

Choicez

How They Impact Our Lives

Aginah Carter-Shabazz

ISBN:061523027X Softcover 978-0-615-23027-6

This book was printed in the United States of America.

To order additional copies of this book, contact:
SULERMAR AND COMPANY, LLC
For book signings email: aginahhair@aol.com
www.thebookchoicez.com or your local bookstore

Contents

Preface 7
Introduction 9
Acknowledgments 11

Chapter One — *Gerri's Story* 13
Chapter Two — *Gerri Meets Gilbert* 26
Chapter Three — *Our Lifestyles Change* 31
Chapter Four — *Club Harlem* 35
Chapter Five — *Brother Lieutenant* 44
Chapter Six — *Sister Aginah* 51
Chapter Seven — *Nas Growing Up* 54
Chapter Eight — *Diagnosed* 57
Chapter Nine — *Hair Biz* 60
Chapter Ten — *Hanging Out* 72
Chapter Eleven — *Nas Meets Hustlers* 77
Chapter Twelve — *My Midlife Crisis* 90
Chapter Thirteen — *Justice for Her* 111
Chapter Fourteen — *Grandmom Leslie* 117
Chapter Fifteen — *JFH Fund-raisers* 131
Chapter Sixteen — *The Trial* 135
Chapter Seventeen — *Trial Transcripts* 138
Chapter Eighteen — *Our Lives After Incarceration* 169

Afterword 173
A Word About Money 175

Preface

I am pleased to write a memoir assessing the lives of ordinary women. This memoir is grounded on revisiting my life choices. My research has been revisiting my life of glamour and violence. My research has led me to an understanding of the connections between persons, places, things, and events. The book speaks to mothers and daughters about CHOICES, about the power of personal vision, and about the reality of our dependence upon each other.

This memoir gives my daughter and me a glimpse of our selves and a reflection of our humanity. And it suggests a model for others to emulate. I hope that reading about our experiences enables you to face hardships you have in your life feeling less alone.

Introduction

Patterns have a funny way of creating themselves. We often feel a sense of youthful reincarnation in the rebelliousness of our children. Our children are but a few steps behind us, emulating our every move. All too often, by the time we recognize where we need to be in life, our children have fallen into pits we have taught them to dig.

I remember visiting my daughter, Nas, in jail as if it were yesterday. I just knew she had to be taking some kind of medication to help her cope with everything that was happening to her because she didn't look like herself. She looked like she was in a daze. My child's life was in slow motion. I could see that she fixed her hair to look presentable, but her mouth was so dry that the corners of her mouth were white and her speech was slurred.

Prison, no matter how many days or hours spent there, is traumatic. You are trapped in a tiny cage, forced to rely on strangers for the basic needs you take for granted until the moment of confinement. Prison closes down your humanity.

How individuals respond to such trauma varies. At the Philadelphia Industrialization Correctional Center, where Nas was incarcerated, prison psychiatrists recognize the pressures inmates feel. Whether guilty or not guilty, during confinement, they are quick to offer temporary relief in the form of extremely strong psychotropic medications.

I can hear her so clearly, "Mom, you can't get me out of here?" I just looked in her face filled with pain.

"Nas, I'm trying to do everything I can to get you out of here. It hurts just to have to come here to see you like this; you know I'm trying my best."

When your children cry out to you that way, you want to do everything you can even if it seems impossible. But I learned from watching my mother and grandmothers that mothers must perform the impossible. Eight years later, Nas' question still echoes. "Mom, you can't get me out of here?"

Like most parents, I have always strived to be someone my children can rely upon, especially in times of dire need. So here I was, staring at my daughter's almost lifeless face, wondering how the possibility of her being on death row became a part of our destiny. I needed to know the answer to this question—for my daughter and for me. The obvious place to look was at my own life. So I looked. It was not easy, but I am glad I looked. I try to convey in this book what I saw. *With Peace and Love, Aginah*

Acknowledgments

I acknowledge God, Guardian, Evolver, Cherisher, and Sustainer of the worlds. We seek help from Him. We believe in Him. We ask forgiveness from Him.

I thank God for blessing me through the following people whose efforts assisted in the preparation of this book. I have many people to thank.

First, there is Dominique London, my assistant and a graduate of Rosemont College, who joined this project in its later stages. She helped me to develop chapters for the manuscript. It is a blessing that we met. She also assisted with the organization of the chapters. In 2006, while I was going through the unanticipated moments and ups and downs of rewriting this story, we helped each other develop a style to connect more directly with the readers.

I owe much to my dear friend, Marilyn Fountain for her outstanding writing skills, her spiritual support and wisdom. She carefully wrote the synopsis for *Justice for Her* documentary.

My deepest thanks go to Dr. Rosa K. Lewis for her loving friendship and therapy sessions once a month at our favorite restaurant. She spiritually helped to nourish me through the good and bad times. She introduced me to several coping skills and helped me to put them into practice in my life.

I thank my friend Stephanie Beyah, a member of my extended family, for her warmth, her courage, her love, and her capacity to give generously to everyone despite their personal circumstances. She is a true "sistah friend." We love and understand each other. One may have friends all over the world, but very few will truly know your heart.

There is no way that I can adequately acknowledge or name the influence of my parents in shaping my life. I thank my dad for his remarkable spirit of survival and his wonderful support. I thank my mother for her courage, her quiet dignity, and her spirit of survival until her death in 1988.

Special thanks to my sister Sheila for her companionship and listening to my daily complaints and for being the best little sister. I thank my niece Sameerah Shabazz for reading the manuscript and making valuable suggestions. And my Aunt Madeline for the support she has shown throughout my life.

My senior great cousins, Ardelia Edwards and Emma Nedra Duval gave lifetime support and love.

Also, I wish to thank my childhood friend Janet Wicks-Benson for our forty-five-year friendship through thick and thin and her all-around helpfulness and her delightful silliness.

I thank you, Valerie Renwrick-Miller and Barbara J. Robinson, for your sisterly influence.

My godmother, Mary Blackwell, has been there for me when times were low and high. She shares her hugs that I desperately miss from my mother who passed away December 1988.

My sheroes: all the hairstylist and shampoo assistants who ever worked at one of Aginah's hair salons from 1978-2007.

I love my client-friends for making me the stylist I am today, for patronizing my salons for ten and as many as thirty years.

There are so many special sistah clients to acknowledge individually for their continued patronage to this very day. *Roll-Call:* Barbara R. (thirty years); Janet B. (thirty years); Gale H. (thirty years); Brenda H. (twenty years); Brenda W. (thirty years); Jennifer A. (thirty years); Yolanda D.(thirty years); Madeline D. (thirty years); Rebecca D. (thirty years); Gerri K. (twenty years); Darlene D. (seventeen years); Deloris R. (seventeen years); Clorise W. (twenty years); Kim G. (thirty years); Joan W. (thirty years); Ordell B. (twenty years); Linda J. (twenty years); Aginah S. (twenty years); Brenda D. (seventeen years); Dene S.; Susan K.; Ami D. (seventeen years); Jennifer M.; Janelle B.; Judy G.; Dr. Claire R. (twenty years); Angie H. (seventeen years); Dr. Safiyya S. (twenty years); Nicole B.; Mary B. (twenty years); Farah Blackwell; Ms. Ruth Thompson (twenty years); Gail Chinn-Pratt (twenty years); Grace S. (twenty years); Linda H. (twenty years); Ramona B. (twenty years); Michelle M.; Michelle T.; Rev. Louise B. (twenty years); Jill; Aisha; Aliyah; Chanel; Latifah; Bianca W.; Jeanette; Gwen A.; Evanna; Sandra; YC; Smiley F. (twenty years); Sieedah; Florence; Paula W.; Dorothy; Mrs. Jean; Ms. Thurla; Ms. Marcella; Mrs. Gloria; Ramona J; Paula H; Rumelle S; Elaine C; and Faye S.(thirty years); Vanessa; Telete; Katrina G. (twenty years); Julia C. (twenty years); Maybelle K. (twenty years).

Last and most significantly, my love goes to Omar; Eric; Aginah E; Sultan III; Anisaa; Jamal; and a newfound love for twin girls, Suhaila and Sameerah. They all have been most loving and demanding of my time with their combined bright faces.

I appreciate the enduring support of my two children, Yonzetta Hudson-Blakeney and Sultan I. Shabazz II.

I salute you all.

Chapter One

Gerri's Story

I remember the summer of my eleventh year when my mom and dad separated. I thought it was the worst thing that could happen to me. It was 1961. Although I agreed to stay in the family house with my dad and my maternal grandparents, I was deeply hurt by my mother moving out to live with her boyfriend. I clearly remember feeling a sense of loneliness and deep sadness because I had to live without both my parents.

I don't remember when my parents fell out of love, but I do remember that one day my mother drove my brother and me to a house we didn't recognize. She told us to sit in the car until she came out. It was safe for children to do that in the '60s. Two hours later, she came out of that house, and I wondered who she was visiting. My mother had been seeing another man, and she made the choice to move in with him. I did not like the choice my mother was making. I made a choice too, which was to stay with my father.

One day my mother came to our house very angry. She had a foreclosure letter in her hand. My father hadn't been paying the mortgage, and they were going to lose the house they had purchased together. My mother pulled out a pistol. She shot at my father as he sat in his red chair watching television. All six bullets missed him.

I didn't actually see my mother shoot at my father, but I was nearby in the kitchen. When I heard the shots I turned around and saw my dad sitting in a frozen position. My mother heard my grandmother coming downstairs from the third floor, and she put her pistol into her purse and left quickly. As she sped off in her Cadillac, my grandmother, a Christian woman, cursed her daughter, calling her a crazy woman and more.

It was a very strange and frightening experience. Those gunshots rang in my ears for many months. I don't know if my mother just wanted to scare my father or if she meant to hurt him. Whatever her intention was, God was with him.

I imagine my father had decided months earlier to stop making the mortgage payments. At first I thought he was not going to do anything to make my mother's life with her new man easy. But who knows why he didn't pay. There was property in his family that would provide a home for him.

A few days after the shooting incident my mother showed up at the house around noon time and demanded that I pack my things and leave with her. She did not give me time enough to pack everything, promising to replace whatever I left with new things, because she was trying to get out of there before my dad came home from work. She explained that we're about to lose the house. When she said that then I knew what the black and white Sheriff Sale sign meant that was pasted to the front door.

My father had not informed me of his plans. Even if he had, I was eleven and not in a position to refuse my mother's demand. I left to live with my mother and her boyfriend, Mr. George. My younger siblings, my brother Monte and my sister Sheila, were already there. The prospect of being reunited with Monte and Sheila made leaving my father a little easier.

Life was changing drastically for our family. We would no longer be the happy family that spent two weeks of every summer in Wildwood, New Jersey, at the summer home of my Aunt Jule. We went to the beach every morning to play in the sand and the ocean. I jumped the waves with my father holding on to me. My brother dived into the waves. We ate the lunch my mom had neatly packed in a brown weaved basket lined with red and white striped cloth. Some days we went crabbing from a bridge. I didn't like that too much. My favorite place was the boardwalk; we walked it every evening so I could eat cotton candy and ride the bumping cars.

I thought about those times as I was about to move in with my mom and Mr. George. I thought about my mom dressing me in adorable little dresses, with a Rothschild velvet trimmed wool princess coat and hat to match, and Shapiro's shoes. I remembered my brother and me watching the Thanksgiving and New Years Day parades from the judges' chambers at Philadelphia City Hall. That was a privilege to view the parade in the warmth of the judge's chambers. I knew those times were gone for good.

After I moved, I communicated with my dad by telephone. I didn't feel neglected, but I felt a deep longing for my parents to be together. Today I know this loneliness caused me to be mischievous to get the attention of my parents since, as I reasoned, being good couldn't keep them together.

Before my parents separated, I was a successful student. My teachers took interest in me because I was hard-working and smart. By the time I was in third grade, I was a star student. I remember at St. Ignatius a teacher named Mrs. Royster, an attractive black woman who had a special fondness for me. She would take me home with her on the weekends because she was friends with my dad's cousin Ardelia. She would ask me to spell a word when no one else knew how. I knew how to spell and had good penmanship. I won many spelling bees. I liked Mrs. Royster very much, and she liked me too. I earned her attention by doing my best in school.

In fourth grade, Sister Mary Dominica Therese chose me for a part in the school's yearly Christmas play because I could memorize my lines before anyone else. When the time of the play arrived, there were students who hadn't remembered their lines, so she gave me their parts too. I was the star of the production.

And to make sure I looked the part, my grandmother Mary (my father's mother) bought me a pair of white and red pajamas with the feet closed in and a top with a white-laced collar. The costume was a hit. I can remember looking out into the audience and seeing my dad and my grandmother Mary smiling and clapping the loudest. I was very expressive saying my lines: "Twas the night before Christmas when all through the house not a creature was stirring not even a mouse."

My parents being separated meant that neither could afford to pay my tuition for St. Ignatius, so after finishing the fifth grade I had to leave. Leaving Catholic school was very difficult, but somehow I had made it through the sixth grade at Blankenburg, my neighborhood public school. Mr. Amos was my homeroom teacher and the music instructor for the school. He too saw my talent and my dedication to school and made a decision about what instrument was best for me. He would always say I was a brilliant student with great potential.

"You belong in the music club." I accepted his decision to play an instrument and I joyfully played the xylophone. I auditioned for and played in the school musical, "Joshua Fought the Battle of Jericho." I received a standing ovation from a huge audience that did not include my parents. I had not told them for fear my mother would not come because my dad was there or my dad wouldn't come because he thought my mom would bring her boyfriend. And my mother's mom, Grandmom Leslie, was physically too big to leave the house unless someone drove her. So, I left the house alone, performed and walked home from my big night at school alone, at seven thirty in the evening, having pretended a ride was waiting for me.

When I started the seventh grade at Sulzberger Junior High my parents had legally separated. I started acting out in school. Being rebellious, not studying, occasionally doing homework, and not completing class assignments kept me in trouble with the teachers. My mom would stop catering to her boyfriend, Mr. George, long enough to go up to the school to see about me. She would get upset and call my dad when I would act up in school. Mr. George received her attention. The very attention I wanted. She would serve

George meals on a tray beside their bed. He ate T-bone steak and the three of us would sit at the kitchen table eating fried chicken breast.

My father reacted calmly to my school problems. "She'll be all right. Don't worry about her," he would say. I didn't see myself slipping, and I knew I would be okay because my father said so. His protection assured me that my mom's concerns were unnecessary, but later I realized they were necessary.

"She'll be all right. Don't worry about her," my father would say.

Despite the school's many complaints, I continued to be rebellious. My counselor recommended to my mother that I see a psychiatrist. She told her I was filled with rage and anger. I recall visiting the psychiatrist at the Child Study Center and having to walk through a tunnel to get to his office. That walk was very frightening. The psychiatrist's office was dark and dreary with a desk and chairs and a bookcase with lots of files lying all around the desk. It was messy.

When the psychiatrist started talking to me I became frightened. He was a strange looking man with a soft sounding voice. I was alone with him. It was extremely uncomfortable being in this room with him. At that second I got a flash back—being sexually molested at eleven years old by a family member. I hurried up, put on my coat, and ran out of his office. I didn't stop running until I was out of the tunnel. I don't know what he told my mother after that incident, but I told her I was not going back there ever again. I made the choice.

Things had come to a point where I needed just one more incident in school for expulsion. The incident came. My eighth-grade English teacher asked me to get the dust pan and brush to sweep the classroom floor as if it were my job. I became defensive. I felt I was being disrespected, like it was above me to sweep someone's floor that I hadn't dirtied. Isn't that how some of us think?

It was the janitor's job, not mine.

"You sweep it your damn self."

He pointed his finger at me and hollered. I thought he was crazy. He started moving desks out of the way, swinging chairs to the side, as if he were going to attack me. We attacked each other until Dr. Young, the principal, came in and demanded that I leave with her. This would be my final incident before being thrown out of Sulzberger Junior High School. Even though my mother was going back and forth to the school, I was still always in some kind of trouble with the teachers, jockeying for attention. Dr. Young called my mother for her to pick me up, but my mother was not home. The principal told me I was expelled.

Carmen, a disciplinary school for girls, was my next stop. Carmen was located near the Richard Allen "projects" at Eleventh and Melon Streets.

I was begging God to please save me; I had heard so many terrible things about that school and didn't want to go. Look at my choices.

"You mean I'm actually going to a school with all those rough and tough girls?"

"Yeah, you think you're rough and tough," my mother said. Later I learned that my mother made several calls and a visit to Dr. Young, pleading on my behalf because she did not want me to attend Carmen. The visit had no effect on Dr. Young's decisions and off to Carmen I went.

Things were not completely bad. Ms. Sylvia, who lived next door, had a niece, Florence, who attended Carmen. Florence stayed with her aunt some nights during the week and we went to school together.

I wasn't as nervous to go to Carmen anymore because my homegirl was there running things. When I arrived at Carmen, I was okay. The principal placed me in a classroom where we didn't even come out of the room for anything. We stayed in that classroom all day. I was okay with that. I was thinking that I would not have to be in contact with other girls. I stayed in that class for one month. While in the "lockdown class," I met and actually befriended girls who were just like me, girls who made and were making bad choices. They weren't so tough.

After taking a placement test at Carmen, I was moved to regular classes. Even though my behavior was the reason I was placed in Carmen, I had never stopped being a bright child. Now I was able to switch classes and go to cooking, gym, and social studies.

I attended Carmen for longer than I wanted, but to be transferred back to regular school I had to have a clean behavior record. I had fallen into the Carmen culture, and good behavior was not valued in that culture. So I remained a bright girl who behaved badly. Looking back I realize that the Carmen experience was less than educational or developmental. In fact, to be honest, it was humiliating.

And there was more humiliation. I became pregnant when I was fifteen. I was expecting a lecture from my mother about premarital sex, but that was not her concern. Her concern was that I had embarrassed her, my family, and myself. Her overall response to the situation was to ignore me. That was the greatest humiliation.

It happened when my mother and her friends went to a show at the Latin Casino in Cherry Hill, New Jersey. Before she left, she said, "I'm going to leave y'all here, but don't go off the porch." Back then, you did not go off the porch if your parents said do not go off the porch.

I wasn't even thinking about boys when Sample, the boyfriend of my girlfriend, Brenda, introduced me to his friend Ronald. I was the youngest in the group, naive and impressionable. Ronald, Sample, Brenda and Pat were thought of as "old heads" because they were older. We also thought they were wiser. We would all hide and sit on the steps up the street from my house on the weekends. I remember one Saturday night two older girls talking to us about sex, "Oh, girl, go ahead and try it; don't be scared.

When my mother left for the show all dressed up, Ronald walked down the street to my house to sit on my steps. He talked me into going inside. We were watching TV, and he started trying to kiss and touch me all over. I must have said, "No no, stop," at least ten times or more.

I kept saying, "I'm scared, no, I can't, it will hurt, no."

But finally I stopped fighting him roughly. I think I could have fought him off but I stopped trying. I was not relaxed at all though. I was scared. I was tense. I was upset that I had gotten myself into this situation. Finally, I stopped crying and he forced himself on me. I felt like I never wanted to see Ronald again.

A month later, I began to feel sick and didn't know what was wrong with me. I was clueless. I shared my fears with my friend Vicky. Her aunt, Ivory, was my next-door neighbor, and Vicky and I were very close like sisters. She would do anything for me. I looked up to her as a big sister. She helped me land my first job as a file clerk at Kelly Girl Temporary Services.

"Well, what do you think? Do you think you're pregnant?"

"Pregnant, how? We only did it once."

I was scared to death when she asked me that question. My heart was racing, my hands were shaking, and I was a nervous wreck.

"Don't worry about it. We'll tell Aunt Ivory and she'll tell you what you need to do. She'll help you get "un-pregnant."

The last thing I wanted to do was have a child. I didn't know a thing about childbirth, and I didn't have a clue what it meant to be a mother. I was a child myself. As I look back on it now, I was not interested in having this child, in order to have Ronald stick around. Sure I was needy, but I didn't believe getting pregnant would make a boy stay with me or that a child would bring us closer together or keep him faithful. If that were the case then my parents would have stayed together.

Ivory sent us to the store to buy dry mustard and some quinine pills. She bought the gin. She told me to drink the glass of gin, take the quinine pills, and then soak in the tub of dry mustard. I was a mess. Because we lived in connecting houses, I had to climb over my porch banister to sneak into my house. I fell right to sleep. I was drunk. I was afraid. I was very sick to my stomach. I did it again the next day, but none of that stuff was working. I didn't even know when I was supposed to have my next period, but my mother certainly did.

"Did you have a period?" she asked.

"Oh yes, I had a period," I lied.

I did not know what to tell her because I was so embarrassed, so afraid and miserable. One day she said I was not looking right. So she took me to the hospital to get examined. Hospital results during those days did not come back immediately. We had to wait for a hospital staff person to call. I do not remember the doctor calling. I do remember overhearing my mother on the phone. She was telling the lady on the other end that she needed her to perform an abortion on her daughter.

My grandmother, Mary, called when my dad told her the news. "If you take my granddaughter to have an abortion and something happens to her, I will have you arrested. She could die. That will not happen." I didn't have the abortion. Unbeknownst to her in 1966 my Grandmom Mary was "pro-life." And for good reason. The backroom abortionists of those times used a catheter and a hanger.

Being pregnant out of wedlock was very embarrassing for my family and painful for me. My mother was so upset that for a while she could not stand to look at me. I was still going to Carmen throughout my pregnancy until one day I was called to the nurse's office.

"Are you pregnant?" the nurse asked.

"No," I answered.

"You need to bring a note in from a doctor stating that you aren't pregnant."

She gave me a letter with instructions and told me to give it to my mother.

I went home and never went back to Carmen.

Here I was fifteen and pregnant, but worse than that I was not going to school. I sat around the house or went back and forth across the street to my girlfriend's house just to be in the company of friends who didn't condemn me. They never talked about the pregnancy because they saw I was always very sad. There were no baby showers for unwed mothers, so there was nothing to look forward to but having the baby. My grandmom Leslie would say, "Baby showers are for married women."

I was making my regular visits to the GYN clinic until I went into labor. I was home at my mother's when I started having excruciating pains. She said that it was time for me to have my baby. She drove me to the Philadelphia General Hospital (where Children's Hospital is today) at Thirty Fourth Street. When I got there, I was given a hospital gown and told to lie on the table to be examined. Being examined every fifteen minutes while in pain and without my mothers presence were the worst. Then the nurse turned me on my side and I was given an epidural to numb the pain for childbirth.

"You must be still when we put this needle in your back," the nurses told me. I was young and scared. I don't quite remember the entire delivery. But I do remember the soreness because I asked the nurse why I couldn't walk. She told me I had twenty-two stitches.

On April 14, 1966, I gave birth to Yonzetta Sytira Hudson. She weighed eight pounds seven ounces. I got her middle name from Ivory. When she found out I was keeping the baby, she told me, and "I know you're giving our baby my middle name, right?"

Yonzetta was a beautiful baby girl. When I brought her home, I treated her like a baby doll. I brushed and styled her hair, bathed her, and spent a lot of time just staring at her. My girlfriends did the same. They were always at my home just to sit and hold her. My mother took care of Yonzetta and bought her so many pink dresses and sweaters that she later began calling her Pinky. She also began arranging for me to marry Ronald.

We got married at my mother's home November 1966. She rented us a two-bedroom house in West Philadelphia. The marriage lasted only three months.

One day, Ronald went to work and I tried to cook a good meal since he had asked two days earlier when was I going to act like a wife should. I had not been cooking for him. My mother brought us food she cooked, or we went to her home to eat. I spent my days washing and folding clothes at the Laundromat, cleaning the house, and visiting my daughter at my mother's home until it was time for Ronald to come home from work.

We were not happy. Ronald often didn't speak when he came home. And when he didn't speak I didn't either. I can't even remember if we ever told each other "I love you" or if there were any yearnings for sex. I didn't know how to be his wife. Being affectionate wasn't natural for me. I had not learned to be affectionate from my mother. She was a provider, but she wasn't affectionate towards her children. Her mother, my grandmother Leslie, wasn't affectionate either. But I knew without a doubt that my mother loved me.

I was alone in the marriage. I didn't have my daughter with me. She stayed with my mother after Ronald and I moved in together. For those three months, I was in another world wanting to be home with my mother. I was somewhere but too young to know where. We needed someone to educate us. I didn't understand Ronald and he didn't understand me. I worried silently, always to myself, never sharing my loneliness with anyone.

I was haunted by my parents' separation during my marriage. I started to wonder if this was how their separation began. There were no conversations. I wasn't enjoying the arranged marriage. I wanted to be with someone who loved me and with whom I could have fun. I was still a child. I wondered how I got myself into this situation. Living with a man didn't work for me. So I thought about how things would turn out for me if I left. I wanted to leave Ronald.

One evening right after Ronald arrived home from work, I told him I was going to the store to buy a loaf of bread. Little did he know I would never come home to him.

I had seventy-five cents to my name. A loaf of bread cost twenty-two cents and public transportation cost fifty cents. I decided that I would use my last bit of money to take the Route 15 trolley car that ran the Girard Avenue line to go back home to my mother's house.

I was back! I sat on my mother's porch with my girlfriends Janet, Yvonne, Brenda and Vicky—laughing and talking and enjoying that girlfriend bond.

My mother was happy I was home even though she didn't verbally express it. She asked me several times when I was going home. But she knew I was home for good. She continued to take care of my baby and me.

My mother, Elizabeth, was young, smart and beautiful with a shapely figure that men would "die for" as they say. She had long, wavy, black hair that she wore in a ponytail. The only time I saw my mother wear her hair out was when she modeled in fashion shows. When she wasn't going out, she was a homemaker who earned her money by saving and drawing interest through many years of investing what was given to her by her common-law husband.

When she was married to my dad, Donald Carter, she worked with his mother, Mary, "living in" and cleaning for a rich white family on what was called the "Main Line." At this time she and her friends entertained on the weekends or went to shows at places like the Latin Casino in New Jersey. They also frequented Atlantic City's Kentucky Avenue on the Northside. It was the '50s and my mother was stylish and beautiful.

I was named after my grandmother's employer, Geraldine Simpson who became my godmother. Mrs. Simpson showered me with expensive beautiful gifts. She taught my grandmom Mary how to shop for the finest clothes, and she taught her about style. Actually grandmom Mary already knew much of what she was being taught. She just needed the money. Recently, my dad gave me the address to that Main Line home on Sabine Avenue. Though Mrs. Simpson doesn't live there anymore, that house still stands today. It looks every bit of what I remember from when I would "sleep in" with my grandmom Mary.

"Lizzy" as she was affectionately called, was the mother who raised Gerri, Monte and Sheila. She lived her life as a fun-loving mom, giver, friend, and homemaker. She always said her job was to raise her children and give them what she didn't have because she grew up in poverty.

Lizzy devoted herself to learning about the inner workings of home-based businesses so she could teach and provide for her children. We wanted for nothing even though she and my father were divorced. She raised us with a firm hand. Though she wasn't especially affectionate, everyone knew her children were her life. Lizzy was a provider, the provider for her mother and father, her siblings, and their children too. She invested her money buying several properties on the block on which we grew up on. She paid cash for them.

My mother was an economic lifesaver who always came up with money from somewhere at the time when her children or family needed it. The most important lesson I learned from her is that you should always have some money saved in the bank. Excellent credit. And also have money put aside and hidden in the pocket of the coat hanging in the closet or under the mattress, money for "a rainy day" for survival.

My Mother
June 30, 1934 – December 14, 1988

My mother died at the age of fifty-four from various maladies related to alcohol abuse. Her alcoholism crept up on her and on me. As a child I saw her drink socially. I also saw what caused her transformation from a social drinker to an alcoholic. I saw her abused emotionally and physically by her common-law husband, the man everyone called "Daddy George."

In the beginning her life and our life with Mr. George was a good one. My mother took good care of him. She washed and ironed. He had a clean, starched, shirt for work whenever he needed one. She cooked his meals, often delivering them to him in bed. And Mr. George took good care of my mother and her children. He made good money as a long-distance truck driver for a meat packing company.

They had fun together. He had money to spend on fun. They took two week vacations. They shared the driving to Canada and sometimes Florida. Sometimes she would ride with him on long drives in his tractor and trailer delivering meat. They often dressed up and hung out in the bars in his old neighborhood, North Philly. My mother was a "social" drinker. Mr. George's drinking was a little more serious than that on the weekends.

Sometimes my mother would return from those bar outings alone. I recall one occasion when she returned home after being out for only a short time. She paced back and forth in her pearl necklace and earrings, black dress, stockings, and high heels. Then the phone rang. I answered. It was Mr. George, drunk to the point of incoherence. I called my mother to the phone, but I stayed on the extension long enough to hear him threaten to "beat her ass" for leaving him in North Philly.

I knew that Mr. George would sometimes get drunk and fight my mother while they were out "having fun." I did not know the seriousness of the problem until a day that my mother came home with a black eye which she told me she walked into the car door. So his threat worried me. I would have to stand by helplessly as Mr. George beat my mother. I went to the window every five minutes or so looking for him. Eventually he did show up, so drunk he had to double-park his brand new Cadillac.

I called to my mother to let her know Mr. George had arrived. Then I began looking for some kind of weapon, thinking I had to do something to protect my mother. I found a broomstick and hid with it behind the door of my bedroom. I heard him stumbling into the vestibule. He hollered up the stairs.

"Lizzy, I'm going to beat your ass because you left me."

Lizzy answered calmly, "Yes, I left you, and that was the last time you are going to put your hands on me."

George continued slowly stumbling up the stairs, cursing and threatening. Lizzy calmly responded to the threats.

"I would advise you to go back out that door because if you don't you are not going to like what I got in store for you today."

George took a few more steps, and Lizzy acted. She had a pistol. She shot him in the leg. George fell back down the stairs in his suit, grabbing his leg. It seemed he was so drunk that he was not fazed by pain. His concern was the blood.

I called my uncle, Joe, my mother's youngest brother. He came immediately. He was a big man, six feet five and at least two hundred fifty pounds. Uncle Joe wrapped Mr. George's leg with a towel to stop the bleeding. He then picked him up and sat him in a chair on the front porch. He told Mr. George to tell the police that he got shot while sitting in a bar when somebody started shooting. If he gave any other account of the incident he would hear from Uncle Joe. The police arrived to take Mr. George to the hospital. The account George gave of the shooting was the one Uncle Joe told him to give.

My mother followed the ambulance to the hospital. She took care of Mr. George while he was there with a busted knee cap shattered by a bullet. She continued to wait on him hand and foot when he was released from the hospital.

About a year after that incident George began seeing another woman. The woman would call the house. She and my mother would get into it.

"Your ass is mine if I ever find out where you live," I heard my mother tell her rival one day. Once I answered the phone when the lady called. I begged her not to call anymore, trying to impress her that my mother was serious about hurting her.

Years later I moved out to live with Malik. I visited my mother almost daily. I would bring her money or an outfit that Malik and I had bought for her. She was always drunk medicating her feelings. Now George was away all weekend, coming home on Sunday nights to prepare for the workweek. She hardly saw him.

My mother was now visiting the "state store" at least every three days. When I stopped by her house we usually sat in her dimly lit breakfast room.

She sipped on scotch and talked almost incoherently. I once went to her bedroom and found she had written "George" in large letters with a magic marker on her carpet. She was in pain.

I was so worried about my mother I didn't want her to leave the house. She gave me five thousand dollars to help me open my first salon, but I really did not want her to come to the grand opening for fear she would be intoxicated.

But I did invite her because I loved and respected my dear mother with all my heart and soul. I bought her a nice outfit to wear. I was prepared to give her a nice hairdo at the salon she helped me to get. This meant taking the hair that use to reach her waist that was now thin strands that could only be worked into a miniature ponytail. She didn't attend after all. (My father was there in support.)

My mother was in treatment for her addiction—but she always relapsed. At one point she weighed barely ninety pounds. Her skin was pale. Her clothes were always clean, but she had gone from dressing glamorous to shabby.

I hated George. I even entertained thoughts of shooting him. I dismissed those thoughts in favor of prayer. I asked God to help my mother and me. I feel God helped me to understand what my mother was going through and what she had been through to bring her to where she was—suffering from a broken heart. Embarrassment was no longer an issue for me. My hatred of Mr. George for his abuse of my mother continued to be an issue for a long time.

I invited my mother to Thanksgiving dinner in 1988. I was on a mission. I had begun to look beyond my mother's disease and to see her as the beautiful and strong person she had always been. I wanted the family—especially her grandchildren—to have the same appreciation for her. "Lizzy" was to be the special guest. She was not to bring anything (unless she insisted). I even bought her a new outfit.

She did not show up. She did not call. I cried a lot that night feeling it was all my fault. I was certain that my mother did not come to dinner because she did not want to be an embarrassment to me and her loving grandchildren. But embarrassment was no longer an issue for me. And the children had been prepared to receive their grandmother as their special guest—as.

Lizzy was rushed to Presbyterian Hospital less than three weeks later. She was diagnosed with upper gastrointestinal bleed. She died there shortly after her arrival.

Elizabeth Glenn-Carter was born June 30, 1934. She died on December 14, 1988—at a young age—at the hands of an abusive man. Mom it is still painful for me to have lost you so young. I wish you were here today so I could know you.

Gerri Carter 1959

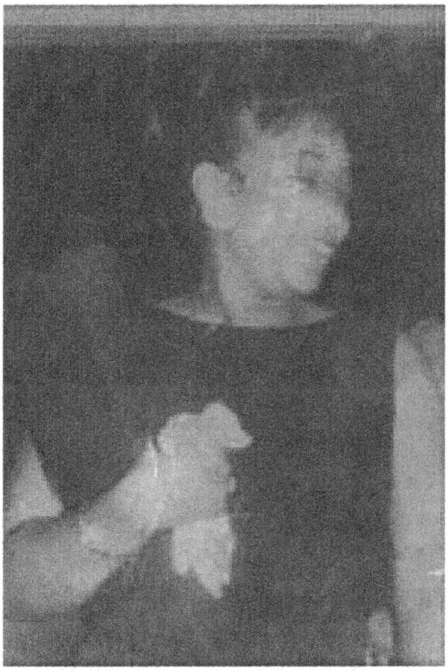

My Mother 1969

Yonzetta(Nas)

Elizabeth Glenn-Carter 1958

Chapter Two

Gerri Meets Gilbert

It was 1968. I was eighteen and longing for attention. I was a teenage mother who had recently walked out of an arranged marriage to a man I hardly knew. I didn't know what I wanted or what I was to do after leaving him other than be with my girlfriends. In those days if a teenage girl had a baby, she married early and settled down to family life like her mother. I knew I couldn't be pinned down to a man I didn't love or even cared much about.

After one year of being separated from Ronald, I met Gilbert, also known as Malik. I met him at the Cadillac Club on Erie Avenue in North Philadelphia. (The Cadillac Club later became the Eldorado Club.) Malik and I began talking, and soon we started dating.

It started with his asking me if we could meet some time. I thought to myself, *I can always meet with you.* Malik was five feet eight inches tall, medium build, with a thick black mustache—and he was bowlegged. I was attracted to him because of his mustache, style of dress, and his bowlegs. His walk was so sexy.

Malik was a very attractive man, probably one of the most attractive men I had ever met. Now, did I say this to him? Of course not! But I was overwhelmed by his masculinity to the point of distraction. Sometimes I had to look away just to pay attention to what he was saying.

Malik had an apartment in Germantown on Mayland Street. I spent many nights there. One night, early in our relationship, somebody was trying to get in with a key.

"Who is that?" I asked.

"Oh shit, let me take care of this," he said.

He went to the door, and I then heard arguing. Soon he returned to the room where I was.

"What's going on?" I asked.

It was his ex-wife. She still had a key, and he had forgotten to change the locks.

"I will change the locks first thing in the morning," he said.

Whatever he said, I believed it. He told me he was going to change the locks. I felt like he was putting a lock on our relationship too.

Months later, he asked me to move in with him, so I did. I moved only my clothes from my mother's house. When I met Malik, my mother was elated. She loved to invite him to our home for dinner. They sat at the dining room table and she listened to him talk about his militancy, his job, and growing up. My mother was crazy about Malik. He was the perfect gentleman, very polite and very caring. They talked a lot. Good conversation puts a mother at ease.

Once when Malik was visiting, Mr. George came home sloppy drunk. He began to abuse my mother for no apparent reason, first verbally and then physically.

Malik told him, "I will not stand here and allow you to beat on your wife."

Mr. George slurred, "Mind your damn business and get out of my house." He slapped my mother again, so Malik karate kicked him to the chest and, in slow motion, Mr. George fell to the floor, gasping for breath, saying, "Okay, I give."

It was embarrassing, but I was overjoyed that Mr. George got knocked down and couldn't get up. Lizzy was very grateful. Believe it or not, Mr. George respected Malik from that day on.

Not many months after moving in with Malik, I began to experience something familiar, something I hoped I would not experience ever again. I would wake up feeling sick. Everything smelled terrible, and I was often nauseous. I started remembering what pregnancy felt like. I began counting the days on the calendar to track my cycle. Then I came right out and said to Malik, "I think I'm pregnant."

We were living in the pre-pill era when birth control was unreliable, abortions were dangerous and illegal, and illegitimacy was frowned upon.

"You think you're pregnant?" he asked.

I got right to the heart of the matter. "I am pregnant!"

"Okay, baby," he said, just the same way he said it when I told him I couldn't get pregnant, like what I said was strange. For some reason I had really believed I could not get pregnant again. I was wrong. And I began to think at that moment, "Here I am, young and careless again." Right away, I knew I couldn't keep the baby. I already had a baby who was only two years old. There was no way I was prepared to bring another child into the world. Malik said firmly that I should have the baby because I was carrying his child. But I didn't feel stable, and I didn't want it.

"You have love, and that's what a child needs," Malik said. But I insisted that I didn't want it. Finally, he said to me, "Whatever you want to do I'll support you."

I had no idea what I should do, so I reached out to friends. I contacted my girlfriend Marion who grew up with me "down the bottom" (if you lived in West Philly below Fortieth Street, you lived in the "bottom"). She gave me the name of a nurse. One of Malik's attorney friends gave him the name of a doctor whose office was in the heart of North Philly. My mother called to make the appointment with the doctor.

Malik and I arrived at a residence that had been converted into a doctor's office. The living room was the waiting area, and what would have been the dining room was the receptionist's area. There were a lot of young women there, all looking scared and confused. Back then there was no Planned Parenthood to give you sonograms to get the exact age of the fetus, no one making you aware of what choices you had—adoption or foster care. There was no paperwork. There were no counselors to help you. I was so afraid, but knowing I wasn't the only one helped.

My appointment was for eleven at night. The doctor performed abortions after regular office hours, one right after the other. Malik went to the nurse's station to ask if we could sign in and come back later. We could, and we went to my mother's house where I felt a sense of security.

We returned to the doctor's office in the wee hours of the morning. Young women were sitting on the steps leading upstairs and on folding chairs in the waiting area. It was dreary looking. There was hardly any lighting.

I don't remember the abortion room. It's a blank for me, but I think it was the room next to the dining room turned secretary's office and nurse's station. I lay back on the bed and placed my feet in the stirrups—I think. I am not certain there were stirrups. I could feel the doctor pushing and probing trying to puncture my womb. It was very uncomfortable and scary, but it wasn't very painful. The pain came later. I remember clearly the ride home. No one said anything.

The next evening, I was experiencing severe cramps. I got scared and called Malik and my mother.

"You're going to have to go back and see the doctor again," my mother said. I learned from the doctor that I had been pregnant with twins. One I aborted leaving his office, and the other I miscarried the next day.

Some days later, I was driving Malik to work and he said to me, "You haven't been yourself since this whole thing happened. You look sad and lonely. I'm feeling real lonely too."

I didn't respond. When he got out of the car, I got out and walked around to the driver's side so I could drive myself home. He grabbed me and hugged me.

"I know, honey, it wasn't the right time," he said.

I whispered, "I can't wait for us to be married so I can have your baby."

That day after work was wonderful. Malik took me to dinner at a soul food restaurant that his boss, Cecil, frequented on Columbia Avenue. I had fried chicken breast, string beans, and sweet potatoes. That night, he kissed me and held me very tight. I felt loved after feeling so empty.

I had been fired from my job as a file clerk at Reliance Insurance Company. Then I was hired through Reverend Leon Sullivan's program to work at a dry cleaners on Diamond Street and then in Progress Plaza. Malik asked me to quit. He wanted me to work with him for the Charles Bowser Recreational Program.

It was my job to visit all of the playgrounds in North Philadelphia carrying a cooler in my car to collect samples of the lunches given to the children that summer. Once I had covered all the playgrounds, I took the samples to be tested for contamination at a laboratory on Walnut Street. After that summer, the program ended because of lack of funding. Malik went to work for the famous civil rights attorney Cecil B. Moore as a paralegal and as a private investigator.

In May 1970, we bought a house and moved from the apartment on Mayland Street to a house on Apsley Street in Germantown. My mother purchased the house in trust for me. That's the only way she would have it. It was a nice two-story, three-bedroom row house that sat on a hill. Yonzetta came to live with us. Malik loved her as if she was his own. He did things for her a father would, and he bought her anything she wanted. She now had her own room with white French provincial furniture and a canopy bed.

I enrolled Yonzetta in kindergarten at the J. B. Kelly Public School, a few blocks away from our home. I dressed her in fancy clothes from Sak's Fifth Avenue and fixed her hair in three double-twist ponytails. I drove her to school every day and picked her up except when the mother of her girlfriend, Christel, picked her up along with her daughter. Christel and Yonzetta were best friends. She also was friends with the Hayes sisters who lived directly across the street from us.

I remember when Yonzetta was five. She experienced one of her best birthday parties. It was in our backyard. Even her Christmas that year was special, as that year, she got her first two-wheeler bike. However, it was her last Christmas celebration, as a child because Malik was militant and a Malcolm X follower, and we began to live by the teachings that Malcolm had been taught by the Honorable Elijah Muhammad. He also wanted me to be a part of the workforce supporting the causes of black people. He first took me to North Philadelphia where I began helping out by serving free breakfast to the children recruited by the Black Panther Party. I liked the idea of feeding underprivileged children, but the building where we did the feeding was cold and I was on my feet for as long as seven hours some days. I soon asked Malik to find me some other kind of volunteer work.

About a year after we settled into our new home, we began to decorate. Of course I was the interior decorator. Malik was impressed with my decorating skills. An interior designer made custom drapes for every room. Red wall-to-wall shag carpet was installed throughout the downstairs. Shag carpet was a '60s thing.

I preferred antiques and traditional-styled furniture because that is what I learned from my grandmother Mary who had beautiful taste in furniture and clothes. After I decorated, Malik bought himself a new blue Coup Deville Cadillac. (Again, my mother was there to sign her name on the dotted line.)

For Valentine's Day, I got a brand-new red and white Grand Prix with white leather interior and front bucket seats. You couldn't tell me a thing. My smile lasted a month, the most I had smiled in a long time. Because of the amount of money Malik was bringing home, we were able to go to New York and "shop on Fifth Avenue."

I remember shopping in the shoe department of Bergdorf Goodman's on Fifth Avenue and spotting Jackie Kennedy wearing a pair of flat shoes and pedal pushers, which today we call capris. She was on the first floor in the shoe department buying shoes. As a young girl, I admired her because she was the wife of President Kennedy. I was especially impressed with what she wore and how she conducted herself so gracefully during her husband's funeral.

I could not believe I was in the same store with her. I moved close to where she was sitting so I could see what kind of shoes she was buying and listen to what she was saying. Her voice was soft. I did not want her to see me staring, so I listened and looked in her direction only when she turned away to speak to the salesman. She asked the shoe salesman to bring out a pair of plain black pumps. He did, and she tried them on and told him to "back them up." She did not pull out a credit card. Nor did she give him any money. She signed her name on his receipt book and left.

I was curious. What did "back them up" mean? I asked the salesman. Of course, he gave me a snotty look. He said it meant that he was to ship pairs of the same shoe in black, brown, and blue. I sat back down and thought, *Wow! One day, I want to be wealthy and sophisticated too.*

That day changed my thinking from just wanting to spend lots of money. I wanted to someday go into an exclusive store for what I wanted and just sign my name on the dotted line. No credit cards, no check, just a signature.

I guess that proves what my grandmother Leslie used to say: "A good name is better than gold." So I started thinking about how I was going to make my name good.

Chapter Three

Our Lifestyles Change

The late 1960s and early 70s was an interesting and powerful period for blacks in America. Martin Luther King Jr. was spearheading the civil rights movement. Malcolm X was the face and voice of another segment of blacks, those who leaned more toward Black Nationalism than civil rights or integration. James Brown impacted people's lives with powerful songs like "I'm Black and I'm Proud!" words that rang out with pride in the black community. It was a wonderful time, one that has left an indelible mark on the consciousness and culture of American blacks.

The era and its causes also had an influence on me. I started wearing a big bush, one influenced by Angela Davis, which I dyed red. My childhood girlfriends, Sheila and Janet, and I all wore red bushes.

Malik, on the other hand, was a militant. He was a devoted follower of Malcolm X. He was intelligent, and he was serious. These qualities made him a valued assistant to the community activist lawyer and politician, Charles Bowser.

Malik's qualities were appreciated by other members of the community, some not as serious about Black Nationalism as Malik. Ty was his childhood friend with whom he had maintained a close association even though they choose different paths. TY was a hustler. Malik was a community activist.

Malik and his friends grew up in a section of Philadelphia called Tioga. They all graduated from Simon Gratz High School. Together we hung out at Club Ciro's, traveled to Nassau and Freeport in the Grand Bahamas, and just enjoyed life. I was twenty-one, and life was great.

Every occasion—my birthday, Valentine's Day, and other special occasions—Malik took me on a trip or bought me expensive gifts: a fur coat, a new diamond ring, a necklace or earrings. I paid no attention to the fact that Ty was a drug dealer and that Malik placed us at risk by associating with Ty and other hustlers. I also made no connection (at least not consciously) between our lifestyle and drug money.

What I didn't see did not concern me. I saw no reason for Malik to abandon his lifelong friends. What I did see is that Malik had a good job working for an attorney. And I saw him as my man who had everything under control.

I never saw drugs in my home, and I was certain Malik never sold drugs. He worked twelve hours a day, so how would he have the time? But I did see money, a lot of it. I didn't make a connection between the money, what Ty was doing, and our lifestyle. I didn't want to think about it. I just enjoyed the lifestyle. I was even able to ignore the risks.

Malik had a license to carry a gun because of the investigative work he did for Cecil Moore, the criminal and civil rights attorney. So Ty asked him to be his bodyguard. Ty was a high school graduate who had smarts enough for college and a profession. Money attracted him to the drug game, but he was not a criminal at heart. He was "too soft for the game" as the expression goes. He was the perfect target for thugs who stuck him up.

Malik's job was to collect and hold money. There were shoeboxes filled with Ty's money in our basement. Malik would bring the money home, count it, and stack it. I would help count. Malik was helping his friend. I was helping my man. Just helping. But like the lunch program, the job became a problem for me—a bigger problem than I had ever had in life.

Ty, Malik, and some friends took a cruise to Jamaica. I did not go. While they were gone, somebody stuck up Candy, a girl Ty paid to stash drugs at her apartment. Candy called me about eight o'clock at night. She was really upset and crying.

"I was stuck up!" she said.

"Oh my god, what happened?" I asked.

"This man stuck me up, oh my god!"

"Who was it? Do you know what he look like?"

"Uh, he had a real thick mustache, wore a black hat to the side, and was driving a black Eldorado. And he took all of Ty's drugs too!"

"You coming up here?" she asked me.

"Yeah, yeah, I'm coming." I really did not want to go, especially with her being scared and my being just as scared. But I felt sorry for her. She could not go to the police, so we really did not know what to do. Then Greg, Ty's friend, called.

"Something happened," I said. "Somebody stuck Candy up tonight."

Greg came to my house and called Candy. She told him what she told me. Greg recognized the stickup man by the mustache and car Candy described. A known drug dealer name Bob. We all waited for Malik and Ty to come back from the cruise. Greg and I went to pick up Malik from Erie Avenue and told Malik what was going on.

"Bad news," I said.

"What? What happened?"

"Candy was stuck up. They took all the drugs."

Malik called Ty off to the side to inform him. Ty put his head down and held his hands to his head. They got in the car, and we took Ty home. Then Malik and I went home. I learned then that Ty had been the victim of extortion a few times by different people.

Malik and Ty phoned each other for a couple of days trying to figure out what to do. Ty's supplier, a "kingpin" from New York, came into town to investigate. He was cursing and carrying on at Candy's house, so I left. It was too much drama for me, and I was scared to death. My stomach was hurting and my teeth chattering. I did not want to be a part of the drama. I did not want to be caught up with people talking about guns and stickups. I did not go to Candy's apartment anymore. She moved soon after that day.

Things began to come clear and unravel at the same time. Shortly after the stickup, Paul, the husband of my friend Shelly, was shot to death. Ty and his supplier believed Paul had his wife Shelly convince Candy to fake the stickup. The supplier had cut Paul off some months back because it was rumor on the streets that Paul was always slow in paying.

My friend Judy, Candy's sister, confirmed this speculation. Because she was Candy's sister, she knew that the stickup had been staged. Bob and the black El Dorado were not in the picture. Paul was very much in the picture. And rumor had it that Ty arranged for Paul to be killed, no doubt at the insistence of his supplier, who had no need for people like Paul being on the streets of Philly. And soft or not, Ty would have to follow orders or he would be out of business. This was the thinking at the time, but it came out later that a "drug boy" from the bottom in West Philly killed Paul for something totally unrelated.

Things had become clear. And things were getting very messy. The night before a planned trip to Atlantic City, Malik came home at four in the morning, explaining he had been working late. This had happened once before. I had been walking the floor, my stomach hurting, feeling certain he was cheating on me. I did not know this for certain, but when he came in I went on the attack, and we started arguing. He began taking off his clothes, and I noticed his under shorts were on the wrong side.

"You've been somewhere screwing somebody because your underwear is on inside out."

"Girl, you're crazy. I got them out of the drawer like this."

"You're a liar. When I wash clothes I make sure I turn them on the right side before I fold them!" I screamed. It was something I learned from my mother. Sometimes I even ironed underwear because that's what she did. I knew he had not put on his shorts on the wrong side when he took them from the drawer. He had put them on in the dark in somebody's house or a hotel room, rushing trying to get out of there before daybreak.

"Guess what? I'm not going anywhere with you!" I said.

"Oh yes, you are," he said. "I brought you a new fur coat and diamond ring to go with your custom-tailored knit suit so we could look good together."

I was not about to go to Atlantic City with him. Actually, I had already decided to leave him. I called Candy because I knew that her boyfriend and Malik had been together. She had not heard from her boyfriend. "Birds of a feather," I thought. Things had become very clear.

Chapter Four

Club Harlem

On Easter Sunday, April 1972, there were about fifteen of us planning to go to Atlantic City for the dinner show at Club Harlem. The club was on Kentucky Avenue on the north side. There blacks had established a powerful economic base in the early 1930's.

Back then, if you were black the white hotels near the boardwalk would turn you away, even if you had a suitcase full of money. But we had a place of our own. We had Kentucky Avenue. You would see a headline like: "Fabulous Club Harlem Girls—performing a couple of dance numbers." The club's entertainment was usually black. You can call it blues, jazz, or whatever you want—the music cooked.

Club Harlem was just one among many nightclubs that lined Atlantic City's most exciting strip, a magical one-block stretch. In those days, you would find huge crowds of both whites and blacks on Kentucky Avenue.

Lots of black men wore "processed" hairdos and colorful zoot suits, with their high waists and wide-legged cuffed pants, with Spectator shoes. Or you might see polyester sport jackets, with the shoestring ties, and pegged-leg cuffed pants. Malcolm X wore zoot suits during his hustler days and he described a zoot suit as a "killer diller." They were a big hit back then.

I never thought about it before writing this book, but my daughter Nas must have enjoyed watching me get dressed up to go out with my girlfriends. It was the same way for me in the late fifties, watching my mother dress up for Club Harlem and other fun spots. She was fabulous. She wore her laced red Carmen Jones dress with rhinestones and matching rhinestone earrings and bracelet. The dress clung to her hourglass figure and flared at the bottom. She also wore red high heels that strapped around her ankles. Before she walked out the door, she put on white dinner gloves up to her elbows, putting her rings on the outside of the gloves the way they did it in her hey-day.

Though the popular hairstyle was either a bouffant or a beehive, where they teased their hair and piled it on top of the head, my mother wore her hair down to her waist. It was long, wavy, and flowing. She looked refined and dignified.

The '60s began with colorful clothes. Women wore miniskirts and hot pants often worn with go-go boots. Men wore polyester pants with the collarless Nehru jacket. Bell-bottomed pants were popular for women in the seventies. And those with nice figures loved the "cat suits," which were designed to show off great figures and make the less-than great appear great. Women wore their hair either short or in a bush. Leather and polyester were the fabrics we wore during those days. Those who could afford it wore gold and diamonds while others wore costume jewelry.

The styles changed with the passing of the decades, but everyone's reason for being on Kentucky Avenue, especially on Easter Sunday, never changed. It was the entertainment. Over the years, everybody who was anybody played Club Harlem, Grace's Little Belmont, and Wonder Gardens: Sammy Davis Jr., Moms Mabley, Ella Fitzgerald, Redd Foxx, Sarah Vaughn, Ray Charles, Sam Cooke, Jackie Wilson, Stevie Wonder, Billy Paul, and Teddy Pendergrass . . . .

It was exciting to be there, especially during the summer season. When you walked down the street, it was like a scene in the movie *Harlem Nights*. The town was bumping. Music was everywhere! People were "strutting their stuff." You could just be on that magical strip, not even inside a club, and you would feel important—like you were playing a part in the movie.

There were lots of businesses: a hair salon on top of Grace's Little Belmont, several restaurants, a hotel, and a cleaners where you could get a shirt ironed for twenty-five cents.

Timbuktu was known for its twenty-five cent drinks. At the Wonder Garden, you could go to shows wearing shorts and a halter-top. But not at Club Harlem. There, you had to be dressed up, and I mean sassy and elegant.

I was in Atlantic City in 2007 with Stephanie, Janet, and Marilyn for Marilyn's birthday celebration. We drove to Kentucky Avenue to see what was left of the famous strip. We were amazed to see Sonny's barbershop still standing at 40 Kentucky Avenue. The past glory of Kentucky Avenue is rekindled annually by Fred Johnson's Summer White Night events at the Atlantic City Museum. Because of it the Kentucky Avenue past will be known to future generations.

Club Harlem suffered a serious blow to its reputation on that Easter Sunday in 1972.

Malik had bought me a black mink jacket that I wore with a two-piece expensive-looking lime green knit pantsuit tailor-made. Tailor-made was the fad. Just about everybody I knew had an original piece of custom-made clothing.

At Candy's suggestion, she and I drove to Atlantic City alone. I don't remember who rode in Shelly's car. Ty bought the tables. Because I was angry with Malik, I was not about to sit next to him. Candy, Shelly, and I sat at the far end of Ty's table, which was in front of the table where Malik and Nate sat.

The show began with Billy Paul singing "This Is My Life." Soon, a well-dressed man approached Shelly and bent over to whisper in her ear. Whatever he said to Shelly caused her to get right up and walk to the bathroom. She looked startled, so Candy and I followed her. She nervously fixed her hair and lipstick, and Candy and I did the same. Not quite sure if I should ask what the hell was going on, I just looked at her and waited for her to tell us something, but she didn't. Candy and Shelly left the ladies' room.

I felt Candy and Shelly were keeping something from me. I stayed behind. I sensed that something was about to happen and my stomach was cramped from nervousness. It was about fifteen minutes before I got myself together and returned to the table.

Soon the man who had spoken to Shelly returned. This time he spoke to Ty. "Steve needs to speak with you outside," he said.

Ty just sat there.

"Ty ain't going nowhere, so if Steve wants to talk, tell him to come in here and talk," Greg said.

I thought about the rumor connecting Ty with the death of Paul, Shelly's husband. Steve was Paul's cousin. He was known on the streets as a cold-blooded killer.

Then I saw Steve. He walked up to Ty. A fight broke out between Greg and the messenger right in front of my table. His name was Lenny. Tables were being turned over. First there were three gunshots. *Bang! Bang! Bang!* From what I can remember I think Lenny fell to the floor. Then lots of gunshots were followed by the three and Ty fell—right in front of the stage where Billy Paul was singing. The gunfire seemed like it lasted for hours. It was like a western or a war movie. I scrambled under a table. Everyone was searching for cover anywhere they could find it.

Then I tried to get up but I couldn't move. A girl was lying on me! I tried to push her off. "Don't move her! She's dead!" someone said. The top of my lime green knit pantsuit was soaked with blood, so much blood that I thought maybe I had been shot. In the dark, I started crawling toward the ladies' room, but I didn't feel any pain, so I realized I had not been shot. I crawled into the ladies' room into a sea of shoes. Then I looked up into a sea of disheveled clothes and mascara-streaked faces. Amid it all was Shelly, looking relatively composed, outfit in tact and not a hair out of place. She had been warned!

The shooting, crying, and panic finally stopped. I could hear the tables being turned over and the police in riot gear hollering. So me and others opened the door and eased cautiously out of the ladies' room. Malik's friend, Nate, shouted at me, "Malik's been shot!" Dazed, frightened, and in shock, I stumbled over to Nate. There was Malik lying on the floor looking like he was dead. Paramedics put him on a stretcher and told me to leave with them and get in the ambulance.

There was a man already inside of the ambulance with his seriously injured wife; she also had been shot. Malik was not dead, but he was unconscious. The man's wife was either dead or dying.

"I was in the service. I fought in Vietnam. I take my wife on a nice outing for Easter Sunday and this is what happens," he said with tears rolling down his cheeks. "When the gunfire started, I grabbed my wife's head to pull her down between my arms for cover. The bullet skimmed across my arm and went right through her head!"

When I arrived at the Atlantic City hospital, I called my mother. "Are you okay?" And in the same breath, "I heard it on the news," she said. "I'm on my way there, be there shortly; don't worry."

In the visiting room, there were many people being carried in that had been shot—men, women, some dead or dying, others wounded and bleeding profusely.

"Is anyone here for Tyrone Palmer?" one of the nurses asked. Greg went up to speak to the doctor.

"Ty is dead," Greg said when he came back over to where I was standing. The hospital emergency area was packed standing room only. I was waiting for someone to come out and tell me Malik was dead. Actually, it didn't matter what they would say or what they were doing. I was just waiting for my mother to arrive.

Some detectives came into the hospital asking questions. They wanted to speak to me to find out exactly what happened. They asked whether if I recognized the shooters. "I'm tired and I'm scared. Please, let me get out of here and if Malik dies, then I will tell you everything I know," I told them.

The doctors had moved Malik upstairs to the intensive care unit. I was just still, petrified. I was thinking that if those gangsters had not killed everyone they wanted to kill, they were going to finish off Malik at some later time. I went up to Malik's room and sat in a chair watching them hook up lots of equipment to his motionless body. My mother and Mr. George came in and began to talk to Malik. He was unconscious.

"You can talk to him; he can hear you, you know," the nurse said. My mother was talking to him, and he moved his legs a little bit and then moved a foot. We were there overnight waiting to see if he would wake up. When I left for home, he was still unconscious. I was extremely upset. And I was afraid.

I knew I had to find a way to get back and forth to Atlantic City to visit Malik. I could not drive. I was too nervous and afraid. Malik had a good friend named Bruce. He picked me up every afternoon and drove me sixty miles to Atlantic City and back although Malik was now in a coma. After my fifth day of visiting, one of the doctors said to me, "You need to get some rest."

One day while at home, worried, scared, and depressed, my phone rang. It was Malik's friend, Gus.

"Yeah?" I said.

"Are you aware that Malik had twin sons?"

"No!" I said.

"Well, I'm calling on behalf of their mother, Jackie. What are you going to do?"

"What the hell do you mean what am I going to do? You better ask Malik what he's going to do when he wakes his ass up!" I hung up the phone angrily. The next time I visited Malik, I questioned him in his coma. I didn't know if he could hear me or not.

"You already cheated on me with one girl the night before you were shot, and now I'm hearing you have twin boys by Jackie. You told me she was a flirt. You told me she was at your job sitting around waiting for Cecil. When Cecil found out, he asked you to keep her out of the office. All of that and she birthed twins, Malik!" I was extremely angry. One of the doctors came in.

"He's in a deep coma, and he doesn't know you're here. We have him on ice packs and life support, and are keeping him comfortable."

"Why is he on ice packs?" I asked.

"So he doesn't get a temperature." Another doctor asked to speak with me in private.

"Your husband was shot twice in the head with two different bullets, a .45 and a .38 caliber that have damaged the front and back of his brain. You look like you're barely making it. I would advise you to stay home to rest and eat. He's not going to come out of the coma from the way things are looking. It's just a matter of time."

One thing I never told anyone was that I was glad the doctors gave me an excuse to stop going to the hospital to see Malik. I was still upset about his coming home at four in the morning with his underwear on the wrong side. Then I find out about the babies he had on my time. Twin boys proved he was cheating—he was a twin himself.

My grandmother, Leslie, called and asked me on the phone how Malik was coming along.

"He's still in a coma," I said.

"If Malik stays alive for nine days, he's going to be all right," she said.

"Grandma, why nine days?"

"Because nine is the number of completion. It takes nine months to bring life into the world and nine days is the number of completion."

For nine days, I was either sleeping away my pain or lying on the carpet in front of the stereo listening to Marvin Gaye's "Mercy, Mercy Me" and "What's Going On" over and over again. On the ninth day, early in the morning, the phone rang.

"Is this the wife of Gilbert Satterwhite?"

"Yes, speaking."

"Your husband has just expired." I didn't understand.

"What do you mean expired?"

"Well, he died this morning."

I started crying hysterically. *Oh my god, he's really gone*, I thought to myself. Even after being upset and having all of those mixed feelings about him, I was in unbelievable pain. I had believed he would survive those nine days and, as cold as it may sound, I wanted him to live so I could question him about the babies. I could care less about him cheating the night before our planned trip to Atlantic City. I wanted the opportunity to question Malik about the babies. So from 1972 to 1974 there was no closure.

I was angry and bitter for months—for years actually. I was only thinking about myself, the pain I was feeling and the loss. I recall Grandmom Leslie trying to console me. She said God kept me alive for a reason. I should be focusing on that instead of what Malik did. I should be thankful God allowed me to live through that horrifying night at Club Harlem.

I tried hard to block out everything about him. I was hurting deep down in my stomach to the point that I couldn't eat or think. I tried hard to block it all out but couldn't. I cried myself to sleep for months.

Soon after Malik died, my mother and I were making arrangements to have him transported back to Philadelphia. The Atlantic City detective came to my home. They took me to police headquarters to question me.

"What happened and who did it? What did they look like?"

"I don't know," I said.

"You said if Malik died you would tell us who did this," one of the detectives said. They were being very persistent without considering the danger to my life. If I didn't know any better, I would have said who I thought had killed Malik and Ty but I had my life and my daughter's life to think about.

"Malik is dead. Who the hell is going to protect me if I tell you what you want to know?" I asked impatiently. Suddenly I didn't know who did it; I don't even remember what they looked like. While they were questioning me, Cecil Moore called.

"If you don't have any goddamn warrant for her arrest, let her the hell go!" He was cursing and screaming, and the detectives were angry as hell because they knew Cecil meant business when it came to his people. My friends were at the house when they came to get me, so they called my mother. She called Cecil.

Cecil Bassett Moore, also known as Cecil B. Moore was a brilliant lawyer and a civil rights activist in the city of Philadelphia. He was light skinned, standing about six feet tall, medium built with curly black hair. He always had a cigar in his hand and was known to drink Old Grand-Dad after he won his cases. He wore skinny neckties and suits with peg-legged pants with cuffs. He concentrated his practice in the North Philadelphia area. He represented or advocated for those who without his help would be "swallowed up" by a system that was both racist against blacks and corrupt generally. And he was effective.

One of Cecil's most remembered achievements was the desegregation of Girard College. Named after an American banker, Stephen Girard, one of America's richest men of his day, the school was built in the 1800s as a school for poor white orphan boys. A ten-foot wall was built around the college, some say to keep these boys in while others claim to keep blacks out. Whatever the reason was, this building that sat in the heart of north Philly's black community began to breed resentment. Legal action went to the Supreme Court four times during the 1950s and 1960s. In 1965, Cecil organized thirty regular picketers, who called themselves, "Cecil's army." Those thirty attracted others. Eventually there were five thousand in the "army" surrounded the school on a particular day as a demonstration. The police commissioner at that time sent at least a thousand officers to disband the picketers. The picketers stood their ground, leading to the desegregation of Girard College.

My mother handled Malik's funeral arrangements, and Cecil Moore eulogized him.

"Tell Mrs. Barkley to make him look like himself again," I said to my mother, giving her a picture to show Mrs. Barkley the funeral director.

On a cold, cloudy Monday, the parking spots on the streets were filling fast. Lots of cars lined up behind the hearse and limousine already waiting at the entrance of the Mt. Olive Tabernacle Baptist Church. After taking a seat with my mother in the front row, I immediately began to look around, scanning the faces row by row. Jackie, the twins' mother, entered the church.

She walked up to Malik's casket with the rest of the people walking by to view his body. She stopped and looked a little longer than anyone else, and she looked as if she were getting ready to lean over to kiss him!

"I dare you!" I said loudly. "I dare you to kiss him!"

"Calm down," my mother said.

"I'm not calming down, that's the bitch that keeps getting people to call my house asking me what I'm going to do about giving her money for Malik's babies. What am I going to do? What is she going to do?" She never did kiss him.

When the service began with singing the opening hymn, I grasped my mother's hand. She put her arm around my shoulders and told me to relax. The Mt. Olive Tabernacle Baptist Church held upper status in the community. That lent weight to the occasion as did a full house of more than four hundred and the eulogy by Malik's boss, civil rights activist and attorney Cecil B. Moore.

"I am sad this morning," he said in a cracking voice with tears running down his face. "I am grieving for my boy, but I cannot, I will not be disappointed today." His was not the typical eulogy, the kind that gracefully struggles to understand the will of God in a merciless world. Cecil used the eulogy to blast the district attorney for connecting Malik to drug dealing. He made comparisons and used the kind of words not used by others who spoke that day.

"My boy was a right-living young man who transcended the corners and did not give his life to drugs and unlicensed handguns. I'm here to bury him who lost his life to a random act of violence. And for once, I do not have to help a young man's family and friends hold their heads high. There was no shame in the life of this fine young man."

Sylvia, Malik's twin sister, recalls the eulogy. The funeral was kind of a blur in some respects to her but there were things that Cecil said that stuck with her, like how Malik was like a son to him and his wanting him to study law, and how he never thought he would be standing there speaking over him. He said that it was probably the first time that a lot of people ever saw him show that kind of emotion. Struggling to hold back tears several times and failing, Cecil called Malik "my boy." Cecil said that he didn't mean "boy" in the way that whites used the term.

"In the twenty five years that he lived, he fought the good fight", Cecil said between sobs. Sylvia said she remembered how Cecil related the story about his falling down an elevator shaft and claiming the reason he survived was that he was wearing a suit that Malik had given him. That suit became his lucky suit.

As he spoke and became more composed, he seemed to really be getting into what he was saying to the point that he misspoke and said, "The people in this courtroom" instead of the "people in this congregation." Funny what sticks in the mind. He said he loved him. Then almost as a relief, the choir chimed in. Then there was the reading of telegrams and messages of condolence, and finally, the reading of the obituary of Gilbert Satterwhite also known as Malik.

At the end of the service, my mother consulted with Mrs. Barkley the undertaker about which family members were to ride in the family cars to the burial site at Rolling Green Cemetery in West Chester.

"Must be one hundred cars," someone in the limo said, as the procession began to roll west on U.S. 1. The Philadelphia Highway Patrol, holding up cars at every stoplight and intersection, escorted the twenty-mile trip.

As Central Scores 9-8 Public League Victory

The Philadelphia Tribu

THE CONSTRUCTIVE NEWSPAPER

5th Club Harlem Victim Is Lai

Moore Blasts DA For Linking Slain Aide to 'Pushers'

Chapter Five

Brother Lieutenant

Five people were killed and fourteen injured in the Club Harlem shooting. Tyrone Palmer (described in the media as "Mr. Millionaire") died the day of the shooting. Malik died nine days later. The other three were innocent bystanders. All were women.

Rumor had it that Black Incorporated was responsible. Black Incorporated was mostly of young black men who had grown up in South Philadelphia. The media sensationalized the group calling them the "Black Mafia." Of course this name began to stick because it raised the prestige of the group in a sense. The media also insinuated an association between this "Black Mafia" and the "Black Muslims," the members of the Nation of Islam. Of course there were NOI members who had grown up in South Philadelphia with men who were now Black Incorporated members, but the connection ended there.

Not too long after the funeral, as the trauma of the events was beginning to subside, more trouble began. Men started coming to my house asking for money and jewelry that belonged to Malik, offering to prevent anything else from happening to me. They would knock on my door and I would scream out the second-floor window that I had given everything away. I called a former schoolmate whose father was a police sergeant in the Germantown section of Philadelphia. He convinced his father to place twenty-four-hour police surveillance on my house for a few days.

One of the Black Incorporated wives, Tanya, called me. She talked about how some detectives told her lawyer that I would tell them who killed Malik if Malik died. I told her that I didn't know what she was talking about. Then she said because of what the detectives told her, I had better be careful because the people who were concerned about what I might say wouldn't have a problem killing me if necessary.

I didn't take her threats lightly. I called a cousin of mine, Rodney Dunn. Rodney was a lieutenant in the Nation of Islam (NOI). I told him what was going on and he told me he would introduce me to his first lieutenant, Brother Gerald—a powerful NOI member.

About a week after I spoke with my cousin Rodney, I finally met Brother Gerald. Rodney and I were at a funeral repast. I was a little nervous about speaking with him because he was a Muslim. It was being said that the Club Harlem shooting was the doing of either members of Black Incorporated or members of the Nation of Islam. Certainly it was Muslim brothers who were harassing me, trying to get me to pay them for protection.

Gerald was intelligent, generous, and nice to be around. He was always teaching. The women he dated adored him and before they knew what had hit them, he had moved on to the next one. "Irresistibly charming" were words women often used to describe him. They loved him, and he liked them.

Gerald was an attractive man with a medium build. He had a smooth and flawless medium dark brown complexion. His hair was wavy without a strand out of place, as though he had it cut every day. He was known for wearing expensive suits, custom-made shirts, and impeccably knotted designer ties. He was popular, and he was well respected in Philadelphia.

In a soft yet firm voice, Brother Gerald said, "How do you know that they are brothers?" I hesitated for a moment, and then I said, "Well, they dressed like brothers from what I could see, with white shirts and bow ties. And they were clean shaven."

He took control of the situation.

"You won't have any problems after today."

He told me I could go anywhere, go out without any trouble. Because he wanted me to trust what he said, he told me to go out and see if anyone harassed me. So I did. That weekend I went to Club Ciro's with my friends. A Black Incorporated member came over to talk to me. I could hardly believe that it was one of the men who had been at Club Harlem! I turned to look right at him, but he didn't seem to notice that the person he was flirting with was Malik's girlfriend.

"I'm not interested in what you have to say," I said.

Somebody called him away from me, and he never came back. My girlfriend was standing near the Black Incorporated member who had called him away. She heard him say to the man that approached me that I was Lieutenant Gerald's woman and that he was not to say another word to me.

For Brother Gerald to command that kind of respect from members of Black Incorporated, he had to wield considerable influence within the NOI. Power within the NOI gave you power outside the NOI in the black community. So now I was stuck with Brother Lieutenant Gerald for his protection.

I appreciated his protection, and I liked him as a person. That was the extent of it. But, as you might expect, he took it further. He began to treat me like I was his woman. I didn't know how to tell him I wasn't interested in him romantically. But he did save my life (and for that I remain grateful to this day).

I couldn't tell him. I didn't tell him. I went with the flow and slowly settled into the relationship. I didn't take the time to learn who he was as a person. I needed a lifesaver, and he needed a trophy. I wasn't patient, and he took charge. I signed a contract without reading the fine print.

Everything about this man was a secret. He would borrow my car for days at a time. Even after he started coming to my house and staying overnight, I still did not know very much about him. I did not know where he lived, what kind of car he drove, whether he was married or how many children he had, or where he worked. I knew nothing about him, and he never did say much about himself or anyone else, either positive or negative.

Gerald always spoke in a pleasant tone with meaningful words. Maybe the fact that he was thirteen years older than me explains why he treated me like I was a little girl. I was becoming more and more shy and introverted. For hours he would lecture my friends and me about the Nation of Islam.

While we were sitting at the dining room table we would go back and forth, almost like a debate about who "I thought I was." As he used my life's story to carefully preached to me about how I should love and respect myself. He always emphasized the need to stop trying to be other than myself, and to dress modestly. This is the message I heard everyday and, I appreciate how his words influenced me to change my lifestyle.

Gerald was one of the wisest and most compassionate men I have ever known. He seemed to know so much about so many things. He came into my life and began ministering to my needs as if he were a professional psychologist accompanying me to levels of understanding I had never journeyed before. I came in touch with my inner self. I made the logical next step and became a member of the Nation of Islam in 1974 (along with my friends, Danita, Stephanie, Marilyn, and Janet). Gerald would have us outside searching the sky for the "mother ship." He was a great influence on my life at that time.

The Nation of Islam had its own private government, and it had investigators. It got back to temple officials that Gerald was spending nights at my house, a violation of the Muslim code of behavior. Because Gerald was an official, they couldn't send the investigator; they sent one of his superiors, Captain David. Captain David (now Da`ood Nasir) came to my house to investigate. When he rang the bell and identified himself, Gerald quietly left through the backdoor.

Had it been determined that he was in violation, he would have been suspended and his punishment would have been the humiliation of sitting through temple meetings in the red chairs in front of the podium facing the congregation.

Shortly after I joined, the Honorable Elijah Muhammad died. His son, W. D. Muhammad, assumed leadership of what became the World Community of Al-Islam in the West (and later the American Muslim Mission). "Temples" became *masjids* (mosques).

Congregation leaders were no longer "Ministers." They were now "Imams." Minister Jeremiah Shabazz appointed Gerald to the ministry. After a short while, Minister Gerald 3X became Imam Sultan Shabazz.

Sultan became the Imam of the mosque 12E located on the second floor at Fifty-Second and Walnut Streets. He was advised that he had to get married. He asked me to marry him. I did on January 18, 1975, but I was not in love with him. I grew to love him very much while in the marriage. (Eventually I learned that Sultan had other children and that he was married to another woman.)

Our wedding ceremony was held at my home on Apsley Street. Many Muslims squeezed into my small row home that day. The reception was at a banquet hall in south Philadelphia, of course, under the direction of Sister Florence (now Florence Ali) and Sister Alma (now Sauda Bey) who prepared all the food mainly to ensure that it would not be contaminated with pork.

Some friends and relatives ridiculed me for marrying a Muslim. My mom refused to attend the wedding. One reason is that I told her that she wouldn't be able to smoke or drink. She showed up at my house after the wedding all dressed up in her blue gown, looking like the bride's mother. Over time, she came to accept and even respect the change I made. She even accepted my abandoning Gerri for Aginah.

Imam Warith Deen Muhammad gave me the name "Aginah." Sultan was a residing Imam; he traveled to Chicago monthly to meet with Imam Muhammad for Quranic and Islamic studies. He returned from one trip with a piece of paper on which the Imam had written my new name. The Imam was responding to a letter I had sent him, asking him for a name. *Aginah* means "promising." You will also find it spelled as *Ajeenah.* Imam Muhammad also named my daughter, Nas. Her complete name is Nasim, which means *soft winds.* My son Sultan, born January 22, 1976, is named after his father.

The transition from a NOI lieutenant to an Imam was difficult for Sultan. Being Imam Sultan Shabazz was not the same as being Lieutenant Gerald 3X. The responsibility was there, but the prestige and power were not. He was no longer a "shot caller." His authority did not rest on his connections and rank in a powerful large organization. He was now a religious leader who had to earn the loyalty of his congregation by meeting their spiritual needs. He represents the best in obedience to the law and teachings of Al-Islam, and he can best conduct the prayer service of the Muslims. People looked to him for guidance and disciplining. There were no captains to monitor his behavior.

In 1980, Sultan got hooked on drugs (free-basing cocaine as it was called back then). He started stealing my money, spending the money set aside to pay bills, and leaving home for days at a time. He crashed his car and started taking mine, leaving me without transportation. I moved out of our bedroom and into my son's room. Then I switched rooms with our son. He went into the room with his father and I put a lock on my bedroom door to keep my husband out. For eighteen months, we were separated living in the same house but sleeping in different rooms.

I started traveling again with my "sistahfriends," Stephanie, Valerie, and Charmaine to Acapulco and Las Vegas and Atlantic City. We were where things were happening. Stephanie and I were in Atlantic City when Resorts, the first casino opened. I remember Stephanie and I took our children. We stayed at the hotel for a week. I recall thinking about what I was going to do about my marriage. I was really unhappy.

When I arrived home from the Acapulco trip, I unlocked the door and saw my husband and friends (Muslim brothers and Greek Mafiosi) sitting at our kitchen table, some free basing cocaine. I announced to the group that I was calling the police, and I did. The detective said because my husband was involved, I may change my mind later, about pressing charges, and they were not going to respond. One of the brothers who was there had the nerve to try to tell me that I was wrong to call the police and out of order for talking to my husband in that tone of voice. My reply was that they were also wrong to be in my home around my son snorting and basing cocaine. I looked at him as if he was crazy!

It was 1980; Sultan was not employed at that time and no longer held his position as Imam. His only source of income was the money that his friends, who were numbers bankers, gave him for providing their operations with protection.

I soon realized he was stealing from our home to support his habit. One day, a man delivered a small bag of groceries from a neighborhood store.

"You owe on your bill."

"Owe on my bill! What bill?"

Sultan had been running a tab at the grocery store. This is how he was eating. I was not sharing the house groceries with him because he was bringing nothing into the house. He was only taking. Once, he took the electric bill money and used it for drugs. Shut-off was prevented by me paying the man who came to do the shut-off. The same happened with the water.

An especially humiliating episode was his stealing a diamond ring from me. Initially, the suspect was a customer, a nice girl from North Philly, named

Deborah. I discovered the ring missing immediately after she left my house after getting her hair done.

Two weeks later, she came back to get her hair done again. An assistant shampooed her. She suggested that I let her pour bleach mixed with shampoo in her hair, but I said no. I did not want to harm her; I liked Deborah. I was upset and wanted to ask her if she took my ring, but I didn't know how to ask her.

My husband had stolen my heart-shaped diamond ring and sold it to a friend to give to his girlfriend. That girlfriend, Sister Jacqui (a Muslim), came to my home one day to get her hair done. She inquired about the ring.

"Did you used to have a diamond ring shaped like a heart?"

"Yes," I said.

"Well, your husband sold it to my husband, and I have the ring."

"You have the ring?" I asked.

"Yeah," she said.

"Well, my husband stole it from me," I told her.

She didn't respond. She got her hair done and left. That was straw that broke the camel's back. He had to go!

His drug problem became worse. He became more abusive. He began to steal more from the house. My sister, Sheila, came to our house one day to borrow a hat.

"Where's your red fox hat?"

"I don't know, probably downstairs in the basement closet."

"You sure?"

I went to look for it and it wasn't there, and a few other things were gone, including my safe and the Kirby vacuum cleaner.

"Your husband sold it to give it to this girl who sells drugs in Germantown. She trades material goods for drugs; and don't act like you don't know your husband is free-basing."

I had to go to court because Sultan had vowed he would not leave. One day after our first court hearing, he tried to take my car keys as I was parking my car. He held on to the window trying to reach over to get my car keys. I was double-parked. I took off, dragging him down the street, zigzagging, while he hung on to the car for dear life. I turned a corner sharply, and he fell into the street. I got calls from people who knew us but didn't know our situation. They were concerned about my emotional state, one that would allow me to injure my husband the way I did.

At the next court hearing, the judge ruled in favor of a separation and Sultan being evicted from the house. I said, "Your Honor, if I tell him to move he isn't going to leave." He said, "Oh yes, he will. I'm going to give you his walking papers."

When I attempted to give Sultan the eviction order, he let it drop to the floor. I called the police as I had been instructed to do in case he did what he did. The police came and escorted him from the house.

The police offered him an opportunity to pack his belongings. Sultan said he preferred to return for them later. I spoke with him by phone and informed him that for two weeks his things would be on the enclosed porch. After that, they would be on the patio outside. I changed the locks. Sultan never returned for his things.

That was the end of my marriage to Sultan. I didn't have to divorce him. My lawyers discovered there was no divorce degree; he was still married to his first wife.

Today Sultan Shabazz is not the Sultan (or Brother Gerald) of twenty-five years ago. He is making better choices. We are friends. For our son, Sultan II, he is a pillar of strength and fountain of wisdom a young man needs to make his way in the world. For our grandson, Sultan III, he is a loving and patient grandpop.

CHAPTER SIX

Sister Aginah

I joined the Nation of Islam in 1974. Gerald convinced me to transfer Nas to Muhammad's University, the Philadelphia NOI grade school. The Muhammad University schools later became the Sister Clara Muhammad schools. Nationwide, today's Sister Clara Muhammad schools are known for excellence. The Philadelphia Muhammad University that Nas attended was good but not excellent. She stayed there for only two years.

I was Geraldine 13X. I enrolled in the Muslim Girls in Training Class (MGT)—directed by Sister Captain Sheila (now Intisar Sharif). I was an enthusiastic MGT student. I also joined the Vanguards, an elite group of sisters specially trained in self-defense and security. Vanguard training was under the direction of Lieutenant Lucy (now Hasinah Shah). Vanguard training also included cooking classes.

As a Vanguard, I stood security at the First National Muslim Bazaar on each of the three days it was held. The Vanguard was on post whenever there was a special event involving Minister Muhammad's "royal family" or dignitaries. Because I was the wife of Minister Gerald 3X, I was at the top of the list of invitees to all special occasions, including dinner with the royal family.

I taught an MGT class, sharing my knowledge about good grooming and beauty problems and how they can become health problems. I wrote articles about hair, skin, and nails for the MGT magazine.

The MGT classes would include many important women such as Sister Elizabeth, the wife of Minister Jeremiah Shabazz.

NOI women were from many walks of life. There were those with bachelor and master degrees and those who had distinguished themselves in business and as entrepreneurs. Women held high positions in the organization. They were doctors, directors of programs, secretaries, and officers (with military titles) who led other women in all aspects of their lives. The religious movement offered a chance for women to learn about their self-worth and to be respected by others as well as themselves while spiritually progressing.

The Teacher of the Philosophy of the Nation of Islam, Master Fard Muhammad, utilized a variety of strategies extracted from the African American Freedom Struggle to formulate the doctrine of the Nation of Islam. This included the Bow Tie, drilling and student lessons of Booker T Washington, the Nationalism of Marcus Garvey, The Mystical Spiritualism of Noble Drew Ali, and the Charismatic Leadership of Father Divine and Daddy Grace.

Although, this approached differed significantly in doctrine from traditional Islam, many of the Nations' practices included how to eat to live, prayer, and dress restrictions which were similar to traditional Islamic teachings.

So the gap between what was called traditional Muslim and members with roots in the Nation of Islam are narrowing as both historical movements are seeing the need to improve the soul to achieve paradise while at the same time being of service and benefit to humanity in particular and the entire creation in general.

Talking about Muslim Unity! The world of Islam can learn from the Nation of Islam's demonstration of unity . . . we were tight, absolutely without a doubt.

So NOI members supported each other in developing and maintaining the regimen required for development and productivity. There were goals, timetables, and schedules. There was a chain of command. Everybody was accountable to somebody. We were productive. The result was that NOI successfully operated its own businesses across America and had economic power.

So, the many reasons why the religious movement had so many followers may have been that the movement gave direction to our lives. We were required to stick to a special diet, no pork, eat one meal a day and to refrain from the use of alcohol, drugs, and cigarettes. Sisters had a strong desire for personal discipline and good grooming. And there were officials who offered support to meet these goals.

Sisters adopted the modest code of dressing exemplified by Sister Clara Muhammad, the wife of the Honorable Elijah Muhammad (and mother of now Chief Imam W. D. Muhammad.) Her usual attire was a white headscarf and a floor-length white dress.

The Honorable Elijah Muhammad spearheaded a unique mode of thinking in the United States during the early 1930s, one that came at a critical period in the development of black people. At a time when many blacks found themselves losing ground and simply unable to hold up under the enormous weight and pressure of poverty, racism, and oppression, Elijah Muhammad captured the attention of blacks by offering them knowledge about and understanding of themselves, putting them on a road to independence and self-reliance.

He taught that despite what we have been conditioned to think and feel regarding who we are and our role in history, blacks were the first scientists and architects of civilization, creating and offering major contributions in the fields of language, literature, mathematics, chemistry, architecture, astronomy, etc. Elijah Muhammad succeeded in improving the lives of blacks, especially the downtrodden, by providing them with spiritual and economic guidance. He gave us a strong sense of identity.

There were great and powerful thinkers, people like National Minister Malcolm El-Shabazz (Malcolm X), Minister Jeremiah Shabazz, and heavyweight boxing champion of the world Muhammad Ali.

These men, influenced by the teachings and leadership of Elijah Muhammad, were strongly committed to improving the quality of life for black folks, redeeming drug addicts, alcoholics, thieves, and prostitutes, and converting people coming out of prison in order to keep them out. Lieutenant Gerald 3X was part of this religious movement.

In March 1975, Chief Imam Wallace Deen Muhammad assumed leadership of the community his father had developed. He made an almost 180-degree turn, teaching NOI Muslims to "keep the good of the old days and bring them with you" as we intensify our study of the Qur'an and the life of Prophet Muhammad, Calling Muhammad Ibn Abdullah the Seal of the Prophets (i.e., there being none to come after him).

Imam W. D. Muhammad is the leader of the largest Muslim community in America. He is an Islamic scholar with keen knowledge of the Qur'an and the Bible and how they relate to our present time. He is an esteemed member of the World Supreme Council of Mosques that is based in Saudi Arabia, the Peace Council, and he is an international president of the World Conference of Religion and Peace. He was a participant at the 1999 Jubillenium Interfaith Conference for World Peace and has met with countless world religious and political leaders over the past twenty-five years, including Pope John Paul II whom he met with at the Vatican in 1996 and 1999. In 1999, Imam Muhammad also addressed a gathering of one hundred thousand at the Vatican.

Malik led me to Islam. Sultan led me to a deeper understanding of the religion. It was not about doing what my man wanted me to do but doing what felt spiritually right. I sought to learn as much as I could and live what I learned as best I could. The Muslim I am today is the result of my learning and living—and, especially, the grace of God.

Chapter Seven

Nas Growing Up

Nas Speaks about Nas

At the age of seven, I was very quiet. I didn't say much at all. My mother says I was introverted. She points to the fact that I never owned a phone book. Actually I didn't need one. The girlfriends I associated with were Deidra Hayes and Christel King who lived on my block, and I saw them every day.

My childhood was plentiful. I didn't have to ask for much. I would have things before I realized I even wanted them. My mother was just that way. She made sure I had the things I needed as well as the things I wanted. My mother even got me things I didn't want. I was comfortable in jeans and a tee shirt, but rarely was I able to dress this way. My mom put me in the clothes she wanted me in because I was a reflection of her and I had to look the part.

She would style my hair in three ponytails that swung a bit below my shoulders. I remember her ironing colorful ribbons to tie around the ponytails. Clothes were never scarce in my closet; I owned clothes I never wore.

Growing up that way, I became accustomed to having things. And even though I didn't need half of the things I got, I developed the desire to have them. Fortunately, at the same time I developed a sense of wanting to share with others. I would have Nadirah's young brothers scrambling on the sidewalk in front of my house to pick up coins I was tossing out the second floor window.

Aginah Speaks about Nas

I was paying an expensive tuition for my daughter at Raven Hill Academy, where she took her first holy communion. Raven Hill closed, and my husband convinced me to transfer Nas to Muhammad's University where she stayed for two years. She returned to private school, this time to Cecilia Academy. I made sure that Nas went to the best schools so she could have the best education. I had always made a point of seeking the best educational experience for her. This held true also for my son who followed her and for my grandchildren.

When Nas reached her teens my story began to play out in her life. She fell in love with a boy named Mark. She met him through my sister, who was dating his older brother. Mark attended Germantown High School. Nas transferred herself out of Cecilia Academy and enrolled at Germantown to be with Mark. To this day, I still do not know how she did that without my consent.

She went to Germantown for a couple of months and hated it. She realized it was not where she wanted to be academically, especially after having attended some of the best private schools in Philadelphia. But Cecilia Academy would not take her back. She enrolled in and completed Gordon Phillips Beauty School.

At age nineteen, after completing beauty school, Nas became pregnant. I took care of her the same way my mother took care of me. I was in the middle of making wedding plans for Nas and Mark, when she went to his apartment one day and caught him in bed with a girl. I believe that was the last day she ever spoke to him.

I made sure she ate healthy and took natural supplements. She gave birth to a healthy baby boy, Omar, on March 2, 1985. The nurses and doctors said that her placenta was the clearest they had ever seen in a young woman.

Nas Speaks about Aginah and Nas

I was just a little girl when Malik got shot. I was across the street at the home of Janet, my mother's girlfriend. I heard the news about the shooting on the radio. I was very fearful of what might have happened to my mother.

I enjoyed watching my mother and her friends get dressed up to go out. I enjoyed their excitement about the fun they were going to have. I enjoyed how glamorous they were. I wanted to be like her, like all of them.

In my eyes, everything about my mother was perfect. She had dark, short, straight brown hair with full bangs and a tapered cut at the back with soft points on the side. All of her jewelry was real. Her clothes and shoes were expensive designer pieces. Her perfume had a fine fragrance. Her skin was bronze, and her pretty young face showed no struggles in life. When you thought of Aginah, you thought about beautiful clothes, diamond necklaces, luxury cars and the best hair stylist in the city of Philadelphia. When she shopped for tables and chairs, that's not what she bought. She bought "fine traditional furniture."

At age twenty, I embarked on the street life. I wanted what had impressed me most about my mother and her friends. In fact, what I remember most clearly about Malik's funeral were all the furs and fine clothes. I wanted to drive fancy cars, wear fur coats, and have all the finer things in life. My mom tried to direct me away from the guys and that lifestyle where what I wanted was to be found. I would say to myself, "Mom, you did it, so why can't I?"

I learned what I needed to know. I knew who I needed to be with to get what I wanted. The good guys were out. They were too easy. No fun. I wanted a "bad boy." I wanted a man who took charge. I wanted a man who treated his woman like his little girl. I knew I was a grown woman, but I chose not to act like one. It was clear to anyone that I was my own person, but when it came to manipulating men, my behavior displayed anything but that. Glitz and glamour was what I wanted, and that was the way to get it.

I was a daredevil living on the edge in the fast lane. I shopped like it was my job, and when I wanted something, I didn't have to do much to get it. Guys liked me, and I could get them to do things for me. It was so much fun. I felt I was being successful at what I had learned from watching my mother. What I did not realize at the time was that my mother worked very hard for all the things she had. She never relied on a man for anything.

Chapter Eight

Diagnosed

I wasn't old. Thirty-three. My face and smooth skin made me appear even younger. But I wasn't well. The years of standing, the fumes from chemicals in closed quarters, the enduring stress caused by bills and personal issues. They all had taken their toll. This is what I thought.

I had a vague but lingering pain in my abdomen. There were frequent severe migraine headaches. And I was always tired and tense.

Nas knew I was sick. She had heard me talking about it with customers, and she was greatly concerned. She let me know she was aware of my illness while we were discussing how to sew in a weave on a clients head. Such discussions are a special joy for us, especially when together we create a new haircut or style. I respect Nas's sense of design and style, and I enjoy passing my skills on to her.

I returned to my doctor's office for test results. "You have cervical cancer." My eyes began tearing, I was fearful. I thought back to the discomfort I used to feel when I was still having relations with my husband.

The doctor began discussing a hysterectomy. I didn't understand what he was talking about, so without any response I got dressed and left the examination room. I told Dr. Corson, who had delivered my son, "I'll be in touch."

I made an appointment to see a different specialist, Dr. Salerno, at the University of Pennsylvania Hospital. He told me I should have a partial hysterectomy, quite different from the full hysterectomy recommended by Dr. Corson.

While driving home, I thought about my mother cautioning me and complaining often about the fumes from chemical products that were clogging my sinuses. My throat was often irritated, and I suffered from migraine headaches. Over the next few weeks, I read and questioned my clients about hysterectomies. I still wanted another opinion. My friend Janet told me about a place she had heard about, Clymer Healing Center in Quakertown, Pennsylvania.

People visited the Clymer Center for treatment from all over the world. It is a naturopathic health center that treats patients holistically. At that time, it had a living facility, health store, and a restaurant on the premises. At my first appointment, Dr. Mikus told me they could help me by first changing my diet. And I had to believe I could be healed.

I was examined with a laser light. There was erosion in my cervix area. Next to the breast, this area is the most common site of organ cancer, and it is from this area that samples are taken for the well-known Pap (Papanicolaou) test.

Dr. Poesnecker says that during childbirth, the cervix must dilate from a couple of millimeters in diameter to the size of a newborn's head, typically a hundred millimeters or more. Shortly after the passage of the child, the cervix must return to its shape and condition before this dilation. Often in this process, small portions of the inner tissue are left exposed and are subject to the various effects of the environment of the vaginal canal. These tissues, bereft of natural defenses, tend to break down and form a type of lesion known as cervical erosion. A common complication of this difficulty comes from the use of the "pill." Oral contraceptives often cause an imbalance, breaking down the normal tissues in the cervix. This not only causes a certain form of cervical erosion, but also often causes a cystic degeneration of the cervix.

The doctor rolled up some cotton into the shape of a tampon. He dipped it into a homeopathic solution, a part of which was geranium. He inserted the cotton into my cervical area where it had to remain for twenty-four hours.

After removing the cotton, I sat in the bathtub and douched with lactic acid. In a healthy cervix, bacilli produce lactic acid. That activity maintains the necessary acidity to keep the vaginal tract clean and normal.

When I first douched, black tissue came out of me! This stuff was really working. Curious, I picked up the pieces of tissue and placed them on the side of the tub to examine it. It was my flesh—corroded.

My first treatment cost me twenty-eight dollars. Believe it or not, twenty-eight dollars! Not the five thousand dollars it would have cost for a hysterectomy.

It was about two weeks before I received my next treatment. As the doctors instructed, I began eating healthier, juicing everything, no red meat, no sugar or junk foods, no juice with artificial coloring. I just ate veggies and took homeopathic solutions, herbs and natural supplements. Also, I didn't use shampoo or conditioners with the artificial dyes. These can be absorbed into the system through the skin pores.

After about three months, I returned to my gynecologist for a follow-up Pap smear test—and the results were negative.

"Where did you go, to the Clymer Healing Center?" my doctor asked.

"Yes, how did you know?"

"Well, it's a trauma center for women." It seems his attitude was that a place like the Clymer center was an unconventional last resort for desperate women. My view is that a doctor offering holistic treatment should be a woman's first stop.

That was the last time I saw that gynecologist. I believe in holistic healing. I have continued going to the Clymer Healing Center. Stephanie and I travel to Quakertown once a month to see Dr. Neville. Dr. Poesnecker and Dr. Mikus, the doctors who treated me initially, both died a year apart in their late eighties. My guess is that they died of old age—not from disease.

During my treatments I recorded in my journal all of the herbal supplements I was taking. This is when I began thinking about how I wanted to incorporate them into a product line to formulate Aginah's Herbal Hair Products.

At the time, one of my clients, a regional manager for the Nature's Sunshine Company, recommended that I should begin taking the brand of herbs and vitamins that she sold; and I did. I also began selling over seven hundred dollars a month to my customers. She asked if I wanted to become a manager for the company so I could earn a higher monthly percentage. I tried managing for about six months. Too much paperwork was involved and doing hair long hours didn't allot me the time. Actually, all I wanted to do was do hair.

I continued selling herbs as a Nature's Sunshine distributor. Everyone began taking HSNW (hair, skin and nails), Garlic with Cayenne, Kelp and Cascara Sagrada—to cleanse the blood and the colon, to enhance blood circulation and, ultimately, to promote the growth of strong and healthy hair.

In 1985 I coined the slogan "working from the inside out"—making the point that hair is fed by your blood stream. The quality of your blood which feeds your hair depends on your nutrition. Natural ingredients from the refrigerator were incorporated into my hair services in 1978, now Gods Herbs. Today I think of myself as a Holistic Hair Health Educator. I do hair not only as a livelihood but also as a service to the community. And I seek opportunities to teach about the holistic approach to healthy hair.

Having made it through the darkness and being grateful for the lessons I've learned, I find myself armed with and strengthened by homeopathic solutions, herbs, and natural supplements. They each possess some form of healing. I am the Captain of my "Health Ship."

Natural Therapy of Gynecologic Problems in Poesnecker, Gerald E. It's Only Natural. Quakertown, PA. (Humanitarian Publishing Company), revised 1996.

Chapter Nine

Hair Biz

It was March 1973, less than a year after Malik's death. I was twenty-three, a high school drop out, and a single parent. My father encouraged me to finish high school by enrolling me at Lincoln College Preparatory School. I went to Lincoln for three terms without getting my diploma. I was distracted.

After Malik's death, I earned my high school equivalency diploma (GED). In the fall of 1974 I was down to my last five thousand dollars from Malik's insurance policy. How am I going to make a living for Nas and myself? I didn't have enough of my own money. I could hear my mother's words over and over again, "God bless the child that has its own."

I married Sultan Shabazz January 18, 1975. The following year on January 22 my son was born. Time was moving fast, and I wanted to begin my career. Even though I hadn't finished Lincoln Preparatory, the courses I had taken prepared me to earn my GED. In the winter of 1977 I enrolled at LaSalle University to study Criminal Justice. I thought about becoming a probation officer like my cousins. While attending LaSalle, I discovered my passion, Cosmetology. I loved doing hair. I began practicing hairstyles on my sister and her friends.

I enrolled at Wilfred Academy Beauty School in the spring of 1978. I found my comfort zone. I attended LaSalle during the day and Wilfred at night. I attended hair shows in New York City. I traveled from house to house doing hair at six dollars a head. I was raising three children, Yonzetta, Sultan and my niece Sameerah. I taught Muslim Girls in Training (MGT) good grooming classes. I also wrote articles on hair, skin and nails for the MGT magazine.

Something had to give and I made the choice to quit LaSalle. I dropped out and put all my emphasis on completing the cosmetology program at Wilfred Academy Beauty School.

Demand for my services grew so fast I no longer had time to go to customers' homes to do their hair. To be productive and efficient I had to have all my customers come to me. In 1979 I bought my first styling chair and shampoo bowl on credit at Blackman's Beauty Supply and created a styling area in the basement of my home.

I was a one-woman show, doing everything myself: shampooing, blow-drying, cutting, and curling. My business grew, and soon I had to take on shampoo assistants. The first was Nadirah who was soon followed by Charmaine Patrice. They were both teenagers. Over the years, most of my stylist and shampoo assistants were teenagers who came from either Dobbins Vocational School, Beauty school, or some other Philadelphia high school. Today some of those assistants and stylists own their own salons. Roll call (from memory so some may be missing): Marquita, Christel, Andrea, Kia, Gina, Shanon, Deneen, Earlene, Monique, Rhonda, Deborah, Stephanie, Arleasha, Karla, Danette, Audrey, Ebony, Annie, Shante, Miriam, Monique C., Lisa, Kiya, Marquita C., and Kianna, Pumpkin, Desiree, Charmaine R., Feanna, Dara, Nesha, and Gerrell.

I had a thriving business as a natural hair care specialist. I used only natural products, some of which were available in my refrigerator. I thought I was making an honest living. Having just started beauty school I had no idea I was in violation of laws and regulations governing beauty shops. When I learned about those laws and regulations, I focused on leaving the basement as soon as possible. I also wanted my house back.

When I started in business, I noticed that our hair always looked dry and brittle. Regular products gave the hair a stuck-to-the-head appearance. It was glued down to the scalp, looking dull and dry with no movement whatsoever. I wanted to see a different look for Black hair.

Out of my refrigerator came the solution: mayonnaise for flaky scalp and brittle hair; egg whites for protein; and peanut oil for sheen. Then fifteen minutes under the dryer and voila! Hair was bouncy, shiny, and in healthier condition. Everybody was like, "Wow". I got so busy that I was doing twenty customers a day, giving them the Aginah look.

The word started spreading around the neighborhood that a stylist by the name of Aginah Shabazz is going back for the future and surprising the cosmetology industry with some ole but tried and true methods for ensuring healthy hair. It's called, "Working from the Inside Out" which means "building strong resilient hair by consuming natural foods, pure water, herbs and natural supplements". This is a philosophy in which I strongly believe.

I had one customer who traveled a great distance to get her hair care from me. She was Barbara Robinson, a nurse. She traveled once a month from Atlanta, Georgia, just to get her done—in the basement. Today she is a dear friend, still a client, and now she travels from Delaware to Philly so I can take care of her hair. My customers loved the way I styled and the way I cared for the health of their hair.

From 1979-1984 people were running up and down my steps using my bathroom. When the last customer left, I had to disinfect the toilet seat.

People would be in my basement all day and night. I recall four social workers; Tish, Gale, Eleanor and Janice from the Department of Public Welfare coming every Thursday after work, sitting with the people lined up on the basement stairs. Sometimes they would have a long wait. On holidays, they would be waiting until four or five in the morning. It would be daybreak, and I would still be doing ten-dollar hairdos.

It's now 1988 and my name is still ringing loud in the community.

"You got to go to Aginah's to get your hair done."

At a club one night a stranger said to one of my loyal client-friends Gerri Kittrell, "Oh, I know who did your hair; Aginah did your hair." Gerri wore a sharp tapered cut and was electric sliding across the dance floor.

"Yes, Aginah did my hair."

And she kept on sliding. Gerri and I still laugh about that today.

Since the early days when I first developed my own kitchen-aid for troubled hair, there have been some changes. I eliminated mayonnaise and replaced it with peanut oil. Mayonnaise doesn't store effectively in a salon, and I found that the natural, unprocessed oils gave the customer what they needed.

My clients loved the results they got with herbal shampoos and conditioners. I wondered how I could create my own line of hair products. I knew what ingredients were working for my clients. I needed those ingredients formulated into things like pomades, shampoos, and conditioners. I needed the help of a chemist. Research at the library led me to the contact information for the company that produced a product I was using.

I called the company and told the receptionist I needed to speak with a chemist because I was having a problem with one of their products. A chemist contacted me. He was a South Eastern Indian whom I will refer to as JG. I told JG my real purpose. He said his company could do for me what I wanted. He said also that he could take on the project, operating under a small company he was about to launch. He offered pricing and a minimum purchase requirement I could not get from a big company like his current employer. We came to terms, and I was on my way to having my own product line.

The process began in 1984 and took about three months. JG and I were on the phone almost daily. I sent him a list of the herbal ingredients I had been using. He had to determine which ingredients would actually blend together in the pomade he was to formulate for me. It turned out that all the ingredients were compatible. However, he was able to formulate pomade in two fragrances, green apple and baby powder. I loved both. I placed my first order immediately.

A couple of months later, I received my first shipment of Aginah's Herbal Pomade at my new salon—Aginah's Natural Hair Salon in West Philadelphia. With much joy, I stocked the shelves with jars of pomade. Aginah's Herbal

Pomade sold like hotcakes. So now I had to increase my next order by adding two additional products to the line—an herbal shampoo and a conditioner. Later, I added a fourth product—a "leave-in" soybean protein spray. Then I started selling Aginah's Herbal Hair Product line as a package.

I learned that you always have to protect your business assets. One of the stylists I had taken under my wing, teaching her what is not taught in cosmetology school, with coaxing from her boyfriend, stole the chemist contact information and he began selling Aginah's herbal pomade to them without my labeling. Another blow came. This time it was from a client. This particular client also contacted the chemist. Except this time, she and her husband put their own company's label on the jars of pomade. This was my product, my formula, and they had it.

I felt betrayed. How could they do that to me? I remember a lawyer friend telling me that what happened to me was part of the way many people do business. Everyone was for themselves. He went on to say what happen was because I did not request that JG give me my formula before I placed the order. I just did not know enough about the business, at that time, to ask for the formula I helped develop. I never knew or even thought that the chemist could take my product and sell it under another name. I just could not do business with him anymore. I was hurt. I was really hurting. I realized I needed to get over the hurt. I know business can be a dog-eat-dog world. I tell myself, "Beware of the sharks." I didn't understand that then, but today I do. If it can happen, it will happen.

I started purchasing herbal hair products from another company. I searched and searched for another chemist who worked with herbal blends. I found a private labeling company in Chatsworth, California, that would formulate custom herbal pomade for me. It cost more—ten thousand dollars more; that was the company's minimum order. I had to send them a sample jar of the original pomade because I did not have the formula.

While taking a marketing class at St. Joseph's University, my professor, who was also the head of marketing for the Campbell Soup Company, taught me that private labeling was the way to go. He learned about private labeling because his company and so many others were downsizing because it was cheaper to have another company manufacture its products.

Eventually I purchased private labeling shampoo, conditioner, leave-in protein, and holding spray. I sold my products on line, in the Bahamas, at hair salons, and health food stores. Over the years I sold to hundreds of customers who got their hair styled at Aginah's Natural Hair Salons.

I plan to re-launch Aginah's hair products. I do own my brand, a brand I built for over twenty-four years. When I do launch the "New and Improved" Aginah's Herbal Products with national customer support, making my brand your product of choice.

It was during this period also that I changed my residence. My son, Sultan, was starting to "act up." One day a neighbor knocked on my door to tell me about the things she saw my son doing.

"Your son is on the corner gambling."

"Gambling how?" I said.

"Yeah, shooting pennies against the wall like dice."

"Not my son," I said.

"Yes, your son."

I ran up the basement steps and ran around the corner trying to find him, but he was gone. He was only ten years old. I knew it was time to move, especially after hearing rumors that my son's dad had been a gambler in his day.

I moved to the suburbs so I could get my son away from the stuff that was now going on in what had been a "nice" neighborhood. I thought he could get a quality education in the suburbs without my having to pay thousands of dollars for tuition.

It was very quiet in my neighborhood. Some clients thought I was out of touch with them because I was living outside the city in a very quiet area. Lots of them would say, "You live in a senior citizen home." My response was, "Its okay. After hearing water running, curling irons clicking, people talking, radios, and phones ringing all day, it felt good to be home in a quiet environment." It was very peaceful.

At about the same time my girlfriend, Janet, recommended I set up a salon in a building owned by her husband. I was reluctant, but it was time. After I moved to my new living quarters, I move my hair business to a new location. Same following, lots of cash, traveling, nice car, home, expensive clothes, and jewelry.

As a young Black entrepreneur, securing loans for my first hair salon was a challenge. Banks would not give me a loan. They would give me a $40,000 car, but they wouldn't give me $40,000 for a business. I thought that was strange. One of the white officers at the bank told me, "Well Wall Street says it's not profitable."

"What are you saying? Black salons are not profitable businesses?"

Nobody would give me a loan. I've always operated on my own money. With financial help from my mother, I opened Aginah's Natural Hair Salon, my first salon at 46th Street in West Philly in 1985. A friend, an awesome contractor made three custom-built workstations and designed arch-shaped mirrors that he hung in front of the stations. Nine months later he returned to remove a wall to build two more stations. Another friend, an electrician, ran all the electrical wiring.

Ninety percent of my basement customers were loyal and followed me to West Philly. I hired two stylists and taught them the Aginah method of doing hair, but my customers always wanted me to do their hair. There was an area for retailing products. We offered lots of unique things. A girlfriend, a Brazilian airline stewardess, brought Belize`, a natural hair relaxer with black color, straight from Brazil directly to my salon.

I traded in my used Mercedes 240D for a brand-new 1985 300SD. I was running back and forth to New York, shopping at Gucci, Escada, Louis Vuitton, Bergdorf Goodman's, Susan Bennis, Botticelli's, everywhere!

A client-friend, Susan Faust, referred Alexis Moore-Bruton. She came to the West Philly grand opening with Susan. Alexis worked for the *Philadelphia Inquirer*. She came in to get her hair done one day.

"I'm doing an article on hair," she said. "Can I write about your salon?"

"Sure," I told her.

She set up the time and date, and her crew came in with cameras and took dozens of photographs. I was given a whole spread in the Sunday *Philadelphia Inquirer*. My girlfriend's husband custom framed the article. It felt good to gain public recognition in your hometown. I was proud of myself.

From the very beginning the salon's clientele included celebrities from all walks of life. Mayor W. Wilson Goode was a regular client.

We worked around the clock at Forty-Six Street. Business boomed. My business in West Philadelphia was doing exceptionally well. The second year 1987, we grossed a quarter of a million dollars. When I met with my accountant and a financial specialist, she was amazed that a black salon in the community was bringing in that much revenue. I didn't know what these figures meant for a new business.

While driving one day, I saw a vacant commercial space on the corner of Chelten and Morris. It had been Darrow's drug store, a Germantown landmark. I called the number on the for sale sign immediately. Sadly, someone had already bought it. That brought tears to my eyes. Someone had beaten me to the punch. The purchaser, a man named Gus, invited me to rent it from him. I agreed to rent it. It was three thousand square feet. I had it gutted, and several contractors were involved in renovating it to my liking.

The West Philly salon was left in the capable hands of my daughter, Nas, who was a licensed stylist, Audrey Freeman was also licensed with a bachelor's degree in business and our receptionist, Darlene Davis.

Yes, there were those who said I was a fool to do that much work to someone else's building. My response was that I could make that money back in less than a year—what did I know back then? Not too much about the real estate business.

Sometimes, you cannot wait for loans. You have to spend your own money. The people at Philadelphia Development Corporation who were involved in the process of securing loans for working capital were dragging their feet. I just canceled my application.

I used the revenue from the Forty-Sixth Street salon to renovate the new salon on Chelten Avenue. The blueprint called for four shampoo bowls for the shampoo area and ten styling stations, a manicure and pedicure area, employee lunchroom, coat room, receptionist and waiting area, office and storage space. The first contractors dragged their feet and always wanted more money. They did not finish. I had to hire a second contractor and then a third to complete the work. At the same time, while renovating the new salon, I was spending over twenty-five thousand dollars for shop equipment. I was paying rent of a thousand dollars a month while renovation was under way. And of course I was paying the overhead for the salon in West Philadelphia and maintaining my bills at home.

After a while, my checks were just bouncing all over the place and it was all too overwhelming. I understood, so I left those checks alone. I did not want to deal with the check system anymore because it was getting me in trouble.

I guess that we were at the Forty-Sixth Street salon for another few years, but there was just so much nonsense going on there because I was not able to be there every day. The young stylist boyfriends were running in and out. Neighbors and customers began telling me what was going on in my absence. One incident did it for me. There was a confrontation with one of the shampoo assistance and her boyfriend; he came to the salon to beat up his girlfriend. During the fight, he broke one of the front panes, I was furious. It was getaway time.

I called my friends in the Bahamas, Dee Dee and Marion to reserve me a room and I jumped on a plane to the Bahamas so I could think about my business and its reputation. I concluded while meditating on the beach and also on the plane ride home that I was closing the Forty-Sixth Street salon even though it was making a lot of money. I could not be at both places. It's time to merge.

Upon my return, I walked into the salon and said, "We're closing. This is the last day." Everybody looked at me as if I were crazy. The stylists were sad. Some were mad as hell but tried to cover it up. Some said they were not going, that they were quitting. "You're not going to Germantown?" I asked. "Germantown has ten stations, enough room for everybody; your customers will come." They stalled around, and eventually a few came and some didn't. New stylists filled the empty chairs.

Aginah's Herbal Hair Products began selling in health food stores, hair salons, and in the Bahamas. I started attending the Bronner Brothers show in Atlanta, Georgia, for the purpose of marketing my products and did very well.

Aginah's Natural Hair Salon 11 opened for business on June 6, 1989 in Germantown—400 W. Chelten Avenue. In our new "upscale" salon there were ten stations, four shampoo bowls, six hooded hair dryers, a room for manicures and pedicures, an employee lounge, and a large waiting area with leather furniture. My dream had come true. I bought a piece of art by Erte called *Dream Voyage*. It represented my dream coming true. "In her dream, a beautiful woman is borne aloft on the back of an exotic bird that represents her limitless imagination, unhampered by boundaries or obstacles, she feels free to pursue her own potential and realize her destiny."

I won the bid for a state contract to supply all state institutions with Aginah's Herbal Hair Products. The contract lasted through 1995.

The salon was featured in several newspaper and magazine articles. Among them was one in the first issue of *Solid Gold*, published by Carlos Paine, and another in the September 1991 issue of the hair magazine, *ShopTalk*.

I began mentoring students in the Philadelphia and Lower Merion school districts and founded PEP (Promising Enrichment Program) a program devoted to developing self-esteem in young women and girls.

The salon served as a site for community development activities. It was a creation of love. Thursdays was "Teachers Day" bringing teachers in for discounted service and an opportunity to interact with each other. Dr. Rosa conducted HIV workshops at the salon. Stephanie and I conducted styling workshop for stylists from area salons.

Rob Schoenbaum called from *American Salon Magazine* to say we were chosen as one of Philly's finest hair salons and that he would like to showcase our salon in the June 1992 magazine issue. This upscale magazine was international. I thought of myself as an A-list hair stylist before this article, but—now I'm known internationally. It felt good to be recognized at this level.

The representative who initiated the article called, saying that his camera crew would be in to take pictures. I asked the entire staff to dress up in black slacks and white blouses, and everyone wore either a geometric-styled haircut or a fancy updo. We also did hairstyles on several models for the magazine to display our work. When the magazine hit the streets, oh my goodness, it was something else for me to be proud of, another milestone. People called and stopped in for appointments from all over Philly. I received letters of congratulations from other stylists nationwide.

In January of 1993, the third year of operation on Chelten Avenue, we encountered an ice storm. The Ice left on the roof over several days caused it to cave in and the salon had to close. When I walked through with my carpenter, I was devastated. Salon equipment and floors were ruined with water damage. Thank goodness, I had another location, but it was not large enough to accommodate the other stylist. We managed. The owner refused to repair the roof. I contacted license and inspection and they issued a fine to the owner. While I was in court fighting for the landlord to replace the roof, I began renovating another salon for Nas. It was three doors up from the salon that had been damaged from the storm. We used the equipment from the salon I closed down in West Philly. Business seemed back to normal on the surface, but I was still hurt from the loss of the salon that I had struggled to open.

Six months later, the manager of an apartment building on the other end of the block called to ask if I would like to rent the three suites on the first floor to operate another hair salon. I liked what I saw because it had the space I wanted. I closed the small salon located in the basement of Park Drive Manor and moved to Park Heights. Nas stayed at her salon at 406 Chelten Avenue. In 1995 she closed her doors and merged with me.

1989-1996

During this period I was a mentor to aspiring cosmetologist and a member of the assessment panel and speaker for the Wharton School of Business's Young Entrepreneurs Program at the University of Pennsylvania. I received a trophy, a beautiful piece of heavy crystal shaped like a book. It sits in my china closet. The inscription reads: Wharton West Philadelphia Project 1990, Aginah Shabazz, Aginah's Natural Hair Salon, In recognition for your willingness to give back to our youth.

In fact, over the years I have received a number of recognitions for community service. I received the State Treasurers Award to African American Female Entrepreneurs. Another was the West Philadelphia Corporation's Leadership & Service Award for Economic Development. I directed and produced an award winning documentary "Justice For Her". In 2004 I was appointed to the State Board of Cosmetology by Governor Edward Rendell of Pennsylvania. From 2005 through 2007 I taught Cosmetology Career Planning to teenage girls at the HOPE Charter High School in Philadelphia. In 2006 I offered a "Day of Beauty" to female victims of Hurricane Katrina housed under Philadelphia Mayor John Streets' relocation program. In 2006 I was nominated for the Anita T. Conner Award of Achievement for Outstanding Leadership. Making It Happen! In the same year Aginah's herbal pomade was sold in the Philadelphia prisons. At the time of this writing I have been nominated to be recognized as one of Pennsylvania's Best 50 Women in Business.

In a fitting tribute to my personal triumph and my professional achievements, I was awarded the 1996 Madam C. J. Walker Award by the National Coalition of 100 Black Women, Inc. I was the first cosmetologist ever to receive the prestigious award. I was chosen not only for my innovative work in the cosmetology industry, but for my "steadfast community service and tireless effort to uplift the social, emotional and psychological conditions of young, Black females" by providing them with positive experiences in the areas of growth and development. And I was also honored for my "unselfish commitment to helping aspiring cosmetologist to find their niche in the business."

From my point of view, I was following the legacy left by the legendary Madam C. J. Walker whom I quote as having said, "I got myself a start by giving myself a start." I feel something happened to me that made me come up with something. I consider myself to be a trendsetter. The girls I've taught can go out and be entrepreneurs—leaders in the field. So, in the tradition of Madam C. J. walker, who changed the world of haircare for women of color and taught them to enhance their natural beauty, a new legacy began: creating beautiful hair the Aginah way, "From The Inside Out."

After battling my daughter's crisis with the criminal justice system I had no energy left to work or even to run the daily operations of my salon. The salon fell upon extremely tough times; I had never experienced so much turmoil. And it didn't help my financial situation when I made a moment's decision to pack up and head out of the salon business in June 2001.

Before I made that final decision, I asked three stylists whom I loved dearly—Christel, Marquita, and my daughter—to take over the business. I offered them the equipment, the name I had built over twenty-five years and hundreds of customers. All I expected was a weekly check. They didn't want the responsibility. I was shocked, but didn't have the energy to sit down with them to discuss the business. That weekend, I began to place price tags on all of the equipment, selling at minimal cost, e.g., fifty dollars for a styling chair. The doors closed on June 6, 2001.

I began as a young, twenty-five-year-old entrepreneur. Then after twenty-five years in the business, I quit the business. As my sister Sheila says, "Yes and now you're just a thousandnaire." A thousand dollars was all I could actually put my hands on at any given time. What did I do with all my money? "You must own lots of land in Nassau, Bahamas, by now." I wish. Now with the payments that went towards my daughter's case, producing the documentary *Justice for Her*, insurance payments, credit cards payments, car payments, and daily living expenses, there's hardly any money left to do anything but eat and sleep. *Tough times y'all*, I said to myself. *Should the millionaires apply for supplemental income? I don't think so, just get back in bed and sleep life away*. And I did exactly that for a very long time, suffering with anxiety depression.

I retired in financial hardship. It took me a long time to realize the real value of money. I was trading my hard-earned cash for the things I wanted right there and then without thinking about security for myself in the future. I guess I was under the impression that I would continue with this trade—do hair for the things I needed. But I'm much older now; I can still do hair but not stand for hours like I did when I was a young girl. It takes much more preparation and I get tired easily.

I had no frame of reference for understanding the kind of money I was making. I was meeting a payroll, paying bills, and providing for my family. It was easy for me to see that I was succeeding. What I did not grasp at the time was my potential. I also did not have a grasp of the risks inherent in business.

Had I thought about these things—if I had known to think about these things!—I would have taken time to learn what I needed to know. I would have been prepared for the unforeseen problems. I would not have created problems for myself. Most important, my current personal financial situation would be a lot better than it is.

Instead I enjoyed myself. I did what I loved doing. I styled and cared for my clients hair. I spent as many as twelve hours on some days doing hair, often because customers insisted I must be their stylist. I should not have spent as much time as I did behind the chair. I should have spent more time managing finances, both business and personal.

Had I been focused more on my business finances, I would have benefited more from my earnings. Because I did not bring questions and ideas to my accountant, the benefit I received from them was minimal. And because I did not realize I was on the threshold of building substantial wealth for myself, I did not seek professional personal financial guidance.

I suspect that professional guidance would have kept me out of New York City and frequent visits to stores like Gucci, Escada, Louis Vuitton, Bergdorf Goodman's, Susan Bennis, and Botticelli's. Maybe I would still be driving my used Mercedes 240D that I traded in for a brand-new 300SD, starting a succession of trade-ins, the 1998 BMW 740i was the last of which I gave back to the bank because I could not afford the payments.

I have not given complete details about the unforeseen problems and the unwise moves. The details are not important. My details cannot be any different from those of any woman who does not do with her life or her business what I did not do. I did not learn about business and money. Consequently, I did not have a personal financial plan.

I speak from the vantage point of someone who has overcome the depression and anxiety she brought upon herself with what she did and did not do. I have taken college courses, attended seminars, and read extensively, all for the purpose of learning what I need to know about business, personal finance, and wealth building. And I underscore my learning by teaching what I know to other women, especially young women. I actively seek those teaching opportunities.

Lots of money had passed through my hands. My business had been the "talk of the town." And I had been the "Angel without wings for everyone." I had been recognized with newspaper and magazine articles. From an introvert with low self-esteem, I had become a confident businesswoman. Then I was broke, in debt, and depressed.

That is no longer the case. I have begun to do battle again. This time I am fully armed. God willing, what happened will never happen again.

LETTER OF APPRECIATION/RECOGNITION

Thank you are two words that are too often unexpressed when a teacher promotes a student or an institution grants a degree to a student. Such is the situation for the many hair stylists that Aginah Shabazz has unselfishly taught and enlightened with her perfected skills and knowledge. This letter is in appreciation and recognition of Aginah for her many accomplishments and steadfast determination. Aginah is acknowledged as a successful African-American woman, who is a prized role model to so many of us, directly and indirectly.

As sole proprietor of Aginah's Natural Hair Salons 1 and 11, Aginah has accomplished what so `many of us only dream of. Her salons have served as a stepping stone for so many cosmetologist to enter a world of opportunity with the assurance of Aginah's background and teachings as a solid foundation. Under her guidance, Aginah stresses the importance of quality products and stylist performance that are letter perfect.

To reach the top in one's profession is a commonly achieved goal. But to shed light on so many others while attaining our goals is even more gratifying. For this we thank Aginah Shabazz and recognize her as a woman of heroic achievements. We wish her continued success and happiness in the future.

NADIRAH and SUSAN
2 HYPE
1990

Chapter Ten

Hanging Out

I was doing hair in the basement when Andrea Shabazz called. She wanted me to go with her to the Sugar Ray Leonard retirement dinner and party in Baltimore, Maryland. Of course, I wanted to go, but she said we had to take the train by 6 p.m. Train? We both had cars and luxury ones at that.

"Why the train?" I asked.

"Because we will be coming home very late and we'll be tired. Driving that time of morning is not safe."

"Okay, great," I said excitedly.

I called a few clients to reschedule them for another day so I could be dressed and ready for Andrea to pick me up and we could get to the train on time.

I went to my closet to find something snazzy to wear. After all, this was a major player in boxing, and I wanted to make a grand appearance.

I was no slouch when it came to dressing up or down. Every piece of designer clothing lay almost perfectly on my shapely small frame. Of course my hair was awesome since my salon was among the best in the business. The horn blew and I walked out to Andrea's car. She was just as glamorous as I was. We complimented each other. She parked at the train station, and we caught the train to Baltimore. Then we took a cab to the Baltimore Convention Center.

The place was filled with celebrities. There were current and former boxing stars. Of course Muhammad Ali was there.

Andrea and I were escorted to the table of Jeremiah Shabazz, Andrea's husband. At the table there was a brother named Omar who was sitting next to a woman. He kept looking at me and flirting. I ignored his overtures, and I declined his invitation to speak with him in the lobby. I thought he was there with the woman sitting next to him. Wife, girlfriend, date, whatever, I don't feed into that kind of disrespectful behavior on the part of men.

I visited the ladies' room. When I came out, there he was.

"So what you trying to do, play hard to get?" he asked.

"No, I just don't flirt with a man who is in the company of a woman."

He said the woman was just a friend, nothing more.

His suit was very nice. Then I looked down and saw his navy blue plastic shoes! I left his company and headed back to the table.

It was one o'clock in the morning and I was tired of smiling. I was sleepy and anxious to leave.

Andrea could not leave until her husband was ready. So I asked her if she could get someone to escort me to the train station. She asked her husband. He wanted me to stay and entertain his friend Omar, but he took me to the train station, and I arrived home at daybreak.

The next day, my client book was full. I was just getting settled in when my phone rang. It was Andrea.

"Omar Ahmad is our good friend, and he would like to know if he could call you."

"I'm not interested. He seems like a flirt."

"Oh, girl, I'm giving him your number. OKAY?"

Omar called, and the first thing he said was that I was playing hard to get—again.

"Maybe I'm not trying to be gotten," I said.

He jumped right in with "When can you come to New York?"

"New York?"

"Yeah," he said.

"I have to work."

"I'll pay you for a workday."

Is he serious? I thought.

"Okay, make me an offer I can't refuse."

"I'll pay you double what you make in a day." That's all I needed to hear.

"What train would you like for me to take?"

I checked the schedule, and the best time for me the next day was at 10 a.m. When I arrived, he was there waiting. We got into his Jeep Cherokee wagon with the wooden doors, which I thought was old, not realizing that it was a classic. We had lunch. Then we went to his jeweler in the Diamond Center in midtown.

"Give her what she wants."

I was standing there thinking that it was all a dream. My brain locked. I didn't know what I wanted. I finally picked a fine eighteen-inch, eighteen-carat necklace with an eighteen-carat heart.

Omar said, "That's my heart, and you have it for the day."

I smiled.

He then took me to the Susan Bennis/Warren Edwards shoe store. I began browsing and spotted those navy blue plastic shoes he had on the night I met him. Those "plastic" shoes were genuine crocodile that cost $1,200. He said he had them in all colors. I was wondering who Omar really was and what he did for a living.

My brain was still locked. I couldn't decide what shoes I wanted, so he took me to Botticelli's and bought me four pairs of crocodile pumps at four hundred dollars each. He bought my daughter a fancy pair of black boots, costing six hundred dollars, and had them shipped to her.

I asked to go to Sak's Fifth Avenue, but he wanted to visit a boxing gym first. There I met his fighter and a few of his friends. By the time we got to Sak's I was feeling a little more relaxed.

I shopped for some things for me. Then we went to FAO Schwartz and bought an electronic game for my son. It was close to 3 p.m. I said I had to get home to attend my son's parent and teachers' meeting. I think I said that because I feared getting intimate was on the agenda. We ate lunch at Joe's Seafood Restaurant, and he drove to the train station. Omar waited with me until the train arrived. As I walked toward the train platform, he handed me a stack of money. All I could say was "Oh my goodness" all the way home.

I was so accustomed to doing and working for myself that the special treatment from Omar "made my day." He called to check to see if I arrived home safely. The next day, he called to ask when he could see me again.

"When do you want to?" I said.

He said, "Soon."

I went back to see him on a Monday, my day off. He picked me up from the train and we went to a Fashion Center warehouse near Twenty-Eighth Avenue. He told me to take the elevator to the sixth floor and ask for a certain woman.

I did. She brought out a three-quarter-length blush-colored fox jacket and opened it for me to try it on. I was looking dumbfounded until she said, "Let me wrap it up for you to take with you." I headed down the elevator and back to the car feeling like I was really special to Omar.

I said, "Thank you," and he smiled.

While we were riding, he asked if I would be his woman. That was too much for me so soon, so I said I would think about it. Then he talked about buying a condo in New York where we could spend weekends together. I began to think he was rich. He drove to another shopping area. We went to a Roche-Bobois furniture store.

"Pick the furniture you want for our place."

It was not my style of furniture. I like traditional, but I had never seen anything like the pieces in the store. It was magnificent. Rich, luxurious, colorful, and curvy. Omar gave the salesman ten thousand dollars as a deposit on the furniture. Yes, ten thousand dollars cash. We hung out all day having a good time, shopping and eating at the best restaurants.

A friend was selling a black mink jacket. I called Omar to ask if he would get it for me. He told her to pick up the money from him when she comes to New York. When I returned to New York the following week, we shopped for a mink hat to match the jacket. I told him he had to buy two mink Jeff caps, one for me and one for me best friend Stephanie. He had no problem with that or anything I asked of him.

Now I was seriously thinking about taking Omar up on his condo offer. After about two months of hanging out, he made plans for me to travel to New York on a weekend. The plan was for me to leave late on a Friday. I was not willing, to either take a train or drive at night. He told me to hire someone to escort me. My godson, Moses, rode the train to New York with me. When we arrived, Omar gave him five hundred dollars. Grateful, Moses smiled and left to take the bus home.

I was so nervous because we had planned for me to stay overnight. I was not ready to be intimate with Omar. I hung my outfit in the closet, and we left to have dinner.

We walked past some maintenance men fixing the lights in the ceiling in the hallway. When we returned, Omar said that someone had been in his room.

"How do you know?" I asked.

"Remember those dudes in the hallway fixing that light?"

"I hid my gun inside the closet in the ceiling. They were the Feds, I bet."

Gun? I became nervous as shit. I couldn't relax. I wanted to go home. I was on the next train back to Philadelphia. I called Andrea and questioned her at length about Omar and how he earns his money. She told me he manages his own boxer and owns a shopping plaza with many stores.

"What kind of stores?" I questioned.

"I don't know exactly, I never asked Jeremiah what businesses Omar owns."

Omar finally called and said, "Damn, you're scary."

"Yes, I am very much so. I almost lost my life ten years ago in a shoot-out and have no plans of ever experiencing that again. By the way, who would go in your room to take your gun?"

"The Feds," he said. "Feds, yeah, the FBI, yeah, federal agents."

"For what . . . what are you involved in I asked."

"I'm being investigated for tax evasion."

I met Omar in Atlantic City a month later at what was billed as the fight of the year. His boxer opened the event. Omar demonstrated he was a serious flirt, but it didn't matter to me. I had sensed it when we first met. And I was having a great time. The place was filled with celebrities. Andrea took pictures of Dick Gregory and me.

I became tired and left the arena to go to the hotel room to rest for a while. I opened the door and found a girl in the room.

"Who are you and how did you get in here?" I asked.

"Omar brought me here to wait for him."

Oh shit, let me get the hell out of here, I said to myself.

"Why you leaving?" the girl asked.

"I ain't staying in there with you, that's for sure." Omar was a flirt. No telling why she was there.

I left with the money he gave me earlier in the evening and his twenty-thousand-dollar medallion with diamonds that I was wearing around my neck and drove back home. The next time I heard from Omar, he was in jail. He wanted me to visit him to discuss my getting back the ten thousand dollar deposit from Roche-Bobois. I sent his lawyer the paperwork.

Years later, Omar sponsored a trip to Las Vegas for my girlfriend and me. The occasion was a Mike Tyson fight. Our hotel and fight tickets were on Omar. We were also chauffeured around in the MGM grand limousine. It was truly a wonderful vacation.

Today Omar and I are good friends. He is an innovative and successful businessman. He contributed generously to my struggle to free Nas. He is the godfather of my grandson Omar, and they have a special bond. Omar and his family are part of my extended family.

Chapter Eleven

Nas Meets Hustlers

Aginah Speaks about Nas

Nas is a stunningly beautiful young woman, the spitting image of my mother. Native American features, light bronze skin, deep-set eyes, and long black wavy hair. Five feet three inches tall with a shapely medium build.

I used to look at her and think how I so much wanted to protect her from the things I had experienced. I didn't want anyone to hurt her or snatch her up into the life I had known. I never considered that maybe she was being "snatched up" into the "life" by her admiration for my lifestyle. Maybe I didn't take time to make clear to her that I came by what I had through hard work. My focus was on the young men, looking to protect Nas from the wolves in sheep's clothing.

When I first saw Rick, he was dressed in designer sneakers, jeans, and a polo shirt. He had pulled up to the salon in a red convertible 560SL Mercedes Benz. He sported a short haircut and his attitude stunk—I'm the man type of guy. I feared he was the kind of person my daughter should stay away from.

Rick was trouble. He was physically abusive to Nas. He even beat her up in the salon while she was eight months pregnant with her first daughter, Aginah E., his child. He beat her because he thought a young man who was standing at the receptionist desk was somebody she was dating besides him.

Nas Speaks about Nas

It was fun having a boyfriend who had a lot of money. Rick being a drug dealer was not an issue for me. I remember we made a spur-of-the-moment trip to Florida to go shopping just so Rick could buy a suit.

I called my mother. "Mom, I'm in Florida!"

"What the devil are you doing in Florida?"

I told her we just got on a plane and left. Rick said he had to get a suit, so we went to Florida.

I was in Florida with no clothes or anything. Rick told me we would buy all new stuff when we got there. We went to Rodeo Drive to shop and he bought me everything I wanted and more. I was loving it!

Looking back on it now, I bet my mom looked at my situation as a rerun of her life. She had already learned the lessons she insisted I learn for myself. I wished I had stopped to ask her advice or listened when she tried to tell me things.

The lifestyle I chose has a price. You have to deal with heartache and disrespect. I spent a lot of time alone or competing for Rick's attention. Rick thought that Money could make up for the time I spent waiting for him or wondering where he was. The truth is that the diamond ring, designer bag, and Gucci heels do nothing for sorrow and heartache. Rick also thought that giving me money and buying me things gave him the right to control my life and do whatever he wanted with his, even if what he did was disrespectful to me.

I was with Rick for almost four years. We had two children Eric born August 16, 1987 and Aginah E. born February 23, 1989. Shortly after the birth of our last child, Aginah E., Rick was arrested for rape. The murder of someone other than the rape victim was added to his charges later. I am certain he did not commit the murder because truthfully he was a coward. And I do not know for a fact that he committed the rape. But his lifestyle involved guns and drugs, and he later could not afford high quality legal representation.

Aginah Speaks about Nas

Then there was Darryl. He was good to Nas and her children, but he was extremely possessive. When she broke off their relationship, he was not able to leave her alone. When she wouldn't answer his phone calls, he threw rocks at her bedroom window to get her attention. He broke a window once. And he held her captive in his apartment.

Nas Speaks about Nas

After Rick came Darryl. He was a nice person. We started out going skating and going to the movies with our friends. Then Darryl got serious. I went along for the ride, but I was with him just for fun.

Darryl was not in the drug-dealing game when we met. He had a regular job. But then the next thing I knew, he "blew up" overnight with all of this money. He was dealing drugs. He told me he realized he had to have money to be with me. I insisted he was wrong. But of course I accepted his money and gifts.

People called me his girl, but I wasn't. We were just friends, and that was it. He would give me money or whatever I asked for, but I didn't want to be known as his girl just yet. Eventually I developed feelings for him, and I was ready to be his girl. It was then that I discovered he had a girlfriend! I told him he had to choose between her and me. He took too long to decide, so I decided for him. I moved on after he gave me an engagement ring.

Things were quiet for a while until Darryl heard I was seeing other people. He still thought of me as his woman (property). He would call, and I would not answer the phone. He would show up at my door and I would ignore him.

Then I let my guard down. I needed money. Being naïve and not considering consequences, I decided one day to call Darryl and ask him for some money. I know I should have left him alone, but I needed money, and I knew Darryl would give it to me. I called him. He said he would give me what I wanted, and I went to his apartment.

While I was at his apartment, my pager went off. Darryl grabbed it. He recognized the number, and he became furious. He flipped out. We argued. He would not let me leave his apartment.

When I left the shop I told one of the stylists where I was going. My mother became concerned when I wasn't there for a client. The stylist told her where I had gone. She called around, got Darryl's number, and called him. When he refused to let me go, she called the police. The police arrived, kicked down Darryl's door, and arrested him. They found guns and drugs in the apartment, so he was in trouble for more than kidnapping me. Because of a technicality, Darryl spent only six months in jail. He was released with a ankle monitor.

After Darryl came Randy. I met Randy on a cold winter day. I was parking my car after shopping for groceries. He drove up my street one way. I didn't know him, but he knew me, and it turned out that we knew some of the same people. I refused his offer to help me with my groceries. At his insistence, I took his number, but it was not my intention to use it.

Some days later, Randy showed up at my job. I was annoyed. I told him he could not come to my job or just show up at my house unannounced. But I did find him interesting. He was nice looking, well spoken, well dressed, and he drove a nice car. He said he was a friend of my mother's husband, Troy, so I figured he was cool. We started talking, but only for a while.

Aginah Speaks about Nas

While Nas was working at her salon on Chelten Avenue, she met Randy. She was taken in by his looks and charm. She didn't know that about two weeks (March 1994) before meeting him, his car had been shot up with him in it. The shooting happened right in front of his mother's house. When

Nas learned about this, she stopped talking to him. She had sworn off being involved with hustlers. It seemed that everything was fine, but it wasn't.

Nas Speaks about the Murder

The night of the murder, my girlfriend Naeemah and I had made plans to go to Atlantic City, but she canceled at the last minute. So I just prepared my three children and myself for bed.

Aginah Speaks about the Murder

Nas called me in the early hours of April 2, 1994. She was frantic. Someone had been killed.

"Randy got shot, mom."

"What!"

"Yeah, he got gunned down right in front of my door."

Nas and her children had been awakened by the shots and red flashing siren lights. A Detective Egenloff knocked on her door. He asked her questions about the shooting, none of which she could answer because she had been asleep. He left, leaving her his card so she could call in case she heard anything.

The next morning Randy's brother called. He wanted to know about a Rolex watch Randy had been wearing when he was killed. Of course Nas knew nothing about the watch because she had not had any contact with Randy. She had nothing that belonged to him. But he was persistent and threatening. He called the next day, so Nas called Detective Egenloff.

The detective sent a car to take her to police headquarters at Eighth and Race Street. Nas called me. I immediately left work and went to headquarters.

"What is she here for?" I asked.

"Your daughter asked us to come get her because she'd been getting telephone threats."

"So what's going on?" I asked again.

What Detective Egenloff told us was traumatic and frightening for me. It was especially so for Nas. Her former boyfriend, Darryl, had been charged with the crime. Apparently, in the two years since their breakup, had Darryl become a cold-blooded drug-dealing killer?

Detective Egenloff explained that the shooting was probably retaliation. About a year earlier, the two had a dispute that ended in Randy Shooting Darryl grazing his head. A year later, in 1995, Darryl went on trial for the murder of Randy. He had been caught at the scene of the crime, but he insisted he was innocent. He was sentenced to twenty years to life in prison.

It could be that Darryl was innocent. In any event, he wasn't going to just accept imprisonment. He either became a jailhouse lawyer or the client of jailhouse lawyers. The law books showed him an opening. He filed a convincing brief, and in 1998 he was granted a new trial.

In April of 1998, Nas was subpoenaed by mail to appear as a witness in Darryl's trial. Nas knew nothing about what Darryl was up to. When the subpoena arrived she did not open it immediately. By the time she did, the date of her required appearance had passed. She called me.

"Mom, I got a subpoena but it's late, like a week late. What should I do?"

I called a lawyer, Andrew Gay, and we met him at court with the subpoena. The judge looked at the subpoena and looked at the signature on the paperwork and said, "I never signed a subpoena for Yonzetta. District Attorney Roger King, Detective Egenloff, do you know anything about this subpoena?"

A black man awkwardly stepped forward.

"No, I do not know anything about a subpoena, Your Honor," he said. It turned out that he was lying and that lying was not the worst of his character flaws.

The black man was Roger King, an assistant district attorney. He was responsible for putting Darryl in jail. In the midst of his 1995 trial, Darryl pleaded guilty to killing Randy Slade. DA King had been producing a stream of witnesses to other crimes Darryl had (or had not) committed. Darryl saw himself being "railroaded." What he saw as his only way out was a plea deal. So he took the sentence for the murder of Randy.

The fact that Darryl was getting a retrial was a source of anger and concern for DA King. He tried hard to get Nas to be a witness at the new trial, wanting her to talk about the kidnapping incident. The subpoena Nas received was bogus. It was DA King's intention to trap her into talking about the incident. Now that she knew what he was up to, she was not going to testify against Darryl. She had no reason to either harm or help Darryl. She no longer had or wanted any dealings with hustlers.

This upset Roger King's applecart. He wanted Darryl in jail for life. The fact that the retrial had been granted was an embarrassment to DA King. The retrial was also a source of concern because of what it might reveal about his methods.

Two weeks after the interview with Detective Egenloff, he and fourteen police officers came into the salon.

"Is Yonzetta Hudson here?" he asked.

"For what? What's going on?" I asked indignantly.

"Is she here?

"No she isn't, and what is this about?" The salon had three sections: a receptionist area, several stations to the left along with my private styling area and the dryer and lounge area, and then more styling stations in the rear. Nas was all the way in the back. The policemen did not see her, and I did not want them to know she was there. I needed to know what they wanted with her.

"Is there a quiet place we can talk?" Detective Egenloff asked.

"Yeah, my office, but you have to tell your officers to wait outside. They're intimidating my customers."

The rest of the policeman went outside to wait and the lead detective followed me into my office.

"What do you want with her?" I asked.

"I have a warrant for her arrest."

"Warrant for what?" I asked.

"Homicide."

"What?"

He told me to tell Nas her house was under surveillance. He would give her twenty-four hours to turn herself in. I didn't tell Nas until the end of the day because she still had customers scheduled. When Sister Emma and I began to tell her, she started crying and screaming, asking what was going on. I felt terrible.

Her son, Omar, went home to get a change of clothing for his mother. She spent the night with my sister, Sheila, probably sleeping very little. The next morning, Sunday, we met Attorney Gay at police headquarters at Eighth and Race so she could turn herself in.

I was allowed to sit and wait with her for two hours. We hugged each other until I was told I had to leave. When I received the first call from her, she said she would be detained from three to ten days while things were being sorted out. Those ten days turned into eighteen months.

Nas was charged—without probable caused as it turned out—on multiple charges, including conspiracy to commit murder. I was distraught. But my distress was not debilitating. It was energizing. I had to free my daughter.

Keane, Sameerah, and Sultan

Gerri, Malik, and Tyrone

Gerri and Malik

Aginah, 1968

Mom, Dad and Uncle Joe

Childhood Friends: Butch, Yvonne holding Nas, Autoria, Janet, Kitty, Brenda, and Florence

Mom, Gerri, and Ronald(first husband)

Gerri

Yonzetta & Lisa

Yonzetta & Aginah

Yonzetta and Lisa

Aginah's Wedding

Sultan(second husband) and Aginah

Marilyn and Yonzetta

Chapter Twelve

My Midlife Crisis

Let's call him JJ. JJ was fine as hell, which I couldn't help noticing the very first time I met him. He was six feet one, slim-built with ridiculous sex appeal. He was captivating. And I was old enough to be his mother. When we met, I was forty-three, a mother of two and grandmother of four, an entrepreneur with a successful business. But I was still full of sadness, secrets, anger and insecurities.

I was lonely but also enjoying solitude. I met JJ. He captured my heart. We married then divorced five months later.

JJ was an ex-felon and professional jewel thief who came into my life. He became my love, soul mate, and my husband. Despite the opinions of others, I chose to love him. He was very thoughtful. He made me think he was someone I could count on. There was just something about him.

I told my girlfriend, Delilah, "I loved everything about him right away." Friends told me to get on with my life. The gossipers said I was desperate, that JJ was much too young for me and not my type. No one had any idea that I didn't know how to stop loving him.

JJ could talk about anything. His talk created a craving for companionship that enabled him to walk deeper and deeper into my heart. I found myself drawn to him more and more. JJ was thoughtful and reliable. He was someone I could count on—I thought. I felt a great burning spark of love that I probably never will again.

I wish somebody had sat me down to show me what the ride with JJ would be like, but no one did. Experience was my teacher. I didn't have a clue then that what I was feeling would soon have me feeling lonelier and more isolated.

What I have come to grips with is that despite what I went through I truly loved this man. Ultimately, the most important lesson I learned, which I think a lot of women fail to learn from such an experience, is not to allow love to cloud the fact that the man hurt me verbally and physically and that

I needed to get away from him. All the love in the world couldn't help or change JJ. That is what I wanted in the beginning. I wanted to change him and feel I had accomplished that goal.

JJ came into the salon one afternoon and told the receptionist he wanted to speak with me.

"There's a tall, handsome, gentleman that just told me to tell you he wanted to speak to you for a minute."

I looked up, and he was standing there nicely dressed. Indeed, he was a tall, handsome gentleman. He had flawless skin and nice hair. His cologne was delicious. It said, "Come follow me."

I walked over to him and he said, "Well, can I speak to you outside?"

"Why can't you talk to me right here?" I said.

"Because everybody's looking at us."

We walked outside.

"Do you know who I am?" he asked.

"No."

"My name is JJ. That's what people close to me call me. I sent you a few messages. Didn't you get them?"

I said, "Oh yes, my god-daughter Terry said something or another."

He started with the compliments and the charming conversation.

"You know, I like your hair."

He did a little chatting. Then he said, "I'd like to take you out."

I was looking at him, sizing him up. While he was waiting for me to answer, he took his hand and wiped something off my shirt, near my breast. I stepped back away from him.

"Whoa, I wasn't trying to touch you," he said. "You had something on your shirt and I was just trying to brush it off."

I didn't say anything except, "Well, I'll let you know another time if we can go out to lunch."

"Oh, you're going to play hard to get."

"No, how about I'm not trying to be gotten," I said.

He laughed and asked for my number. I gave him the salon number. Then I gave him a business card to the salon.

"Call me."

He tore it up.

"I don't want a business number. I want your home number."

"I'll give it to you another time. I'm not ready to give it up," I said.

"What do you think I'm going to do with a number? You know your number ain't all that private."

"Maybe you're used to the girls you know giving out their numbers just because you look good. I'm not giving you my home number right now."

When I got back, people in the salon were asking me all kinds of questions.

"Who was that slim goody?" someone asked.

"He's the nephew of my sister's girlfriend Shirley," I said.

"Well, what did he want?"

I told them that he wanted to take me out.

"Whaaaat? Those young guys surely dig you."

So I said, "You know they're toy boys and kind of fun to play with."

JJ called the shop two days later.

"Are you ready to give me that number?" he asked.

"I'll give it to you when I want to, not because you say so and not right now."

He called another day when it wasn't too busy, and I spoke with him for an hour. He liked talking on the telephone. He started talking about when he first saw me. He said he first saw me at The Library, a club in Bala Cynwyd, right off City Line Avenue.

"I was a real young kid then," he said, "probably about thirteen."

"Really," I said.

"I always said to my homey that you were going to be my woman some day. I remember you as clear as the diamond ring on my finger. I used to see you driving a white Mercedes and wearing those Alpina sunglasses. Sometimes you would wear white ones, and sometimes you would wear your black ones, and you always wore a real sharp, short hairdo."

He even described an outfit along with the shoes. Oh goodness, either I looked really good or this man was a stalker or both. Silly me, I was impressed. I wondered if people really paid that much attention to me. I became frightened when it occurred to me that people might be paying that much attention to me without my knowing who or why.

It seemed he had studied me over some years. He remembered some things that I did not even remember. Finally I gave him my home telephone number, not feeling certain he still wanted it. He did.

He called often, and we would talk into the wee hours of the morning—3:00 or 4:00 a.m. I would fall asleep sometimes. Or I would hang up. And he would call right back.

We were really getting to know each other by phone. He was friendly and seemed very kind and caring. I became curious about what he did for a living.

One night, Delilah and I went to a cabaret-themed party with one of her business partners. I mentioned to JJ that I was going. When Delilah and I left the party, he was outside standing by my car.

"What are you doing here?" I said.

"I have something for you."

He went to his car to get a gift he had for me. It was a Judith Leiber bag.

"I see these all the time at Sak's Fifth Avenue," I said. It had little pink crystals. Oh, it was gorgeous and had a barrel-like shape.

Delilah said, "Oh, Aginah, it is gorgeous."

She went on and on and kept looking at him. "He's got taste like that?"

"Yeah, I guess he does."

"You know how much Judith Leiber bags cost?" he said.

Of course I did—three to four thousand dollars. I thought that was a lot to pay for a gift for someone you have known barely a month. But I was thrilled with the bag. When I arrived home, he called. We talked until daybreak. He said he wanted to take me out. I agreed. We went out to dinner. I forgot the name of the restaurant, but it was a five-star. After dinner, he drove me home and asked if he could come in.

I hesitated, but then I said, "Sure, you know you can come up for a little while."

"You're really a snob," he said.

"No, just cautious."

It was one o'clock in the morning. I was tired and wanted to jump into my pajamas and go to sleep. I came out of the bathroom after changing into my pj's and found that JJ had removed all his clothes and was in my bed. Well, I did not know what to say or how to handle that. That had never happened to me before. I didn't question him, allowing him his manhood. I slid in next to him, not touching. He slid his leg close to mine, and I felt what I needed—warmth. He leaned over and kissed me, and I said, "Good night."

"Oh, so I guess it's all right to spend the night," he said.

"Well, you know you can sleep on that side and I'll sleep on my side."

"Why did you put on pajamas?" he asked.

"Because I sleep in pajamas."

"But you've got a man in your bed now."

He started touching me and I told him not to.

"Well, can I hold you?" he asked.

I fell for that and allowed him to hold me until he started taking off my pajamas pants. I protested.

"Oh no, you invited me here, and I'm in your bed butt-naked, and you mean to tell me we're not going to have sex?"

"No, we're not."

JJ jumped up, put on his clothes, and stood in my face.

"You know what—I ought to smack the shit out of you for humiliating me like that."

I was a little afraid. "I would advise you not to do that because it wouldn't take long for the Lower Merion police to get here if I picked up that phone and called downstairs to security. As a matter of fact, I don't even have to pick up the phone. If I scream loud enough, security will be here."

"You know what, you're probably right, and I don't want to be locked up in Montgomery County Prison," he said. He told me over and over how I embarrassed him. He could see I was afraid. He finally left.

He called me when he got home. I told him I did not feel like talking. I really did not want to talk to him. "Please, please, please," he begged. Then he started apologizing.

"I'm sorry for talking to you like that." But I didn't want to have anything else to do with him.

"I was supposed to take you to New York tomorrow," he said.

"Uh huh, I know."

"Are you going?"

"No," I said harshly.

"Why not?"

"Because I'm not going."

"I've got all this money I put aside to spend on you."

I said, "It's okay. Find somebody else."

I had no intention of going to New York with him, and I didn't. I went to a hair seminar that I had planned to go to anyway. While I was at the seminar, he kept calling my mobile phone until I turned the phone off.

That night, he called me at home. "You turned your phone off all day. I couldn't reach you. You're one of a kind and playing hard to get."

"No, I'm not."

"Well, can I make it up to you?"

"No no, you don't owe me anything. Just leave me alone."

I didn't hear from him anymore. Weeks later I was at a hair show. A man approached me, introducing himself as JJ's friend.

"Can I speak to you for a minute?" I didn't want to talk to his friend either, but I did.

"Don't be so hard on me. I just want to deliver a message."

"Okay. What's the message?"

"JJ says he's just so sorry he said the things he said to you. He says he knows it scared you, and that you're not that kind of woman, and that he shouldn't have talked to you like that."

"I appreciate that," I said.

"He wants to call you."

"He has the salon number."

"You know you're the best thing that has ever happened to JJ. He's just all messed up and a confused young man. Please talk to him for me."

The friend called me at work the next day to make sure I would talk to JJ. "When he calls me, I'm going to call you. Please talk to him." I agreed.

The called turned out to be a "hook-up." JJ was in jail. He made a collect call to his friend. His friend called me on a three way.

The call was mostly about how sorry he was for the way he had treated me. Nothing about why he was in jail. Before I knew it, he was calling my job every day, all day. He was using the "hook-up." His friend must have had quite a phone bill.

I had to put a stop to it. "You can't call me here all day like that. I have to work."

"I called there and they told me you were busy."

I said, "I am busy, so that's what they'll tell you."

Then he started asking to visit him.

"Come see you in a jail? You must be kidding, Aginah Shabazz visiting somebody in a jail? Oh no, somebody might see me."

"See you? Wow, you're really deep."

I said, "I am?"

"Yeah."

Over the next six months he continued to plead with me to visit. I finally agreed. He was in Montgomery County Prison. I waited in line wearing dark sunglasses so that no one would see me.

"Oh, you're really trying to disguise yourself. You were serious about people seeing you come here, right?" he said.

"Yeah, I'm serious. I don't want my clients to see me coming to see anyone in a jail."

We talked at some length. It was a pleasant visit. He was talkative and I kept asking what he had done. He said somebody had accused him of stealing and that he had not done it.

I said, "Oh, okay." Then I said, "Stealing drugs?"

"No. If I was a drug dealer, would you have come here to see me?"

"No!"

"Well, why did you say that?"

"I don't know; I'm just trying to figure out what you do because now you're in jail."

"Guess," he said.

"No, I can't guess."

"Well, it has something to do with jewelry. I go to work like everybody else goes to work."

Then he said, "Have you ever seen me with fives and tens and ones?"

"No."

"Whenever you have seen me with money, I had crisp hundred dollar bills, just like they came off the printer."

I asked, startled, "You're a counterfeiter?"

"No, baby. Crisp hundred dollar bills because that was my pay."

I still couldn't figure out what he did. I was full of questions about him and prison life. He told me he got in trouble in Saks Fifth Avenue. He was arrested after leaving the store. Some girl he worked with had told detectives he stole something and he got locked up.

I went back a second time to see him. On that visit, I told him I couldn't come back there anymore. I was feeling sorry for him and liking him at the same time. The guard announced that visiting hours were over. I left with the intention of never returning.

Then he started calling, and he kept calling. He told me his baby's mother came on whatever day she came and that I would have to come on Sundays because she doesn't want to come on Sundays anymore. Now I was learning about his baby and his baby's mom.

He called. "Why didn't you come?"

"Well, because first of all I don't like going to a prison. And then you're going to tell me I can't come the day that I put aside to come because your baby's mother is coming that day. So it seems to me that she is in your life and has first preference, so let her visit. I really don't have to visit, and to be honest, I must have lost my mind to have visited you in the first place."

JJ was very upset, but I didn't go back there anymore. Soon, they moved him somewhere far away, Waymart Correctional Institution. He called and wanted me to visit, meaning I would have to drive for hours if I wanted to visit him.

I refused. "And why are you still calling me?"

Eventually, his begging worked. I gave into sympathy—and my loneliness. It was something to do. I was just working all the time, not seeing anybody.

It was a relationship. Better, I thought to myself, than the relationships of many people who have never seen the inside of a jail. Certainly better than the marriages I had seen end in divorce. So what did I have to lose?

Finally I took the drive to visit him. I enjoyed the visit. I was feeling this man's pain and liking him more, and I liked the stuff he was saying. Also, I liked him because it seemed like he genuinely loved and cared for me. So I visited him occasionally. One time, he was "in the hole." I didn't know what the hole was.

"You mean you're in jail and you get locked up while locked up?"

This was crazy. I went to visit him in the hole because I wanted to see him and see what the hole looked like. He was in a hole, but you did not go to the hole to visit. You went downstairs in another part of the jail. The guards put you in a room with only a table and two chairs. He was at one end of the table and I was at the other end. It was scary being in this secluded part of the jail.

When I left him, I had to walk through the prison and there were inmates in the halls as I passed with the guards. I was scared to death. That was probably how the guards wanted you to feel so you would not want to visit anymore. It worked. I said to myself, "Oh no, never again. I cannot do this."

However, I did do it again **and** he was not in the hole. I went because I really wanted to see JJ's face and because a friend of his wanted me to bring his girl in so they could get married. I drove Deborah to the prison, and she got married. I didn't go anymore after that.

Soon, JJ was writing to tell me he was coming home and that he wanted to marry me. Marry me? For what, I was thinking.

I also thought about the phone bills. He had to call collect from prison, and he called day in and day out. The phone bills ran between $1,000 and $3,000. I talked very little. He was the talker and I was a listener. In those days, he could talk for three or four hours, hang up, call back, and talk some more and I was just listening, being entertained. He told me all about his life as a child. He always had interesting stories to tell.

I was in love with JJ, and I was sure JJ was in love with me. Of course, loving and being in love are two different things—not something I gave much thought to then. I thought more about my need for an emotional physical presence in my life. In fact, I had given the relationship a lot of thought. I concluded that JJ would make a wonderful husband. And I thought about his potential as a salesman for my haircare products. I rationalized that he was in jail because of the choices he made as a teenager.

The day JJ came home we had dinner at the Adam's Mark Hotel. When we were having dessert, he said, "Aginah, in case you don't remember my saying this, I'm in love with you. I want to marry you." I felt panic.

"JJ!"

"Aginah!"

"JJ—why don't we go away to the Bahamas together?" his face lit up.

"Does that mean yes?"

"We'll see. Once you spend time with me you probably won't want to marry me."

He laughed. "Nothing in the world could keep me from wanting to marry a woman I longed for all my life. So we were first married in the Islamic tradition. You've made me one very happy young man. Let's go to the Bahamas in August for our honeymoon."

I nodded my head yes. "I wish it were my birthday, May 13."

He smiled and whispered in my ear, "I promise you that our marriage will last forever."

"Can I kiss you?" he asked, moving closer to my face. "Yes, of course." And I raised my body upward to receive his kiss. He kissed me like we were one.

But not being the aggressor in bed that night, I felt sick with excitement. I wondered, would I make him happy in bed? They say it's like riding a bike—once you do it, you never forget. Maybe he's going to be disappointed in me in bed. Maybe I should just stop worrying about it and enjoy the ride.

That night while we lay there, he suggested that being married in the Islamic tradition only helps us to see if it would work for us.

JJ's reaction to the matching wedding rings I chose gave me the feeling he was sincere. We went to a store owned by a friend of his. I chose a gorgeous baguette with really clear diamonds. It was fairly expensive, but I reasoned that it was the correct match for JJ, a handsome, sharp-dressing ladies man. JJ agreed.

About two months after this, he said, "I want to be married in the court system because I don't want you to just up and walk out of my life."

So we chose Yerkes Wedding Chapel in Upper Darby for the ceremony. Yerkes is where my mom and dad married in 1949. The day we went there to be married—oh my goodness, I don't know what happened. I can't remember what I said or what happened to cause him to snap. But snap he did. He banged on the car's dashboard until it cracked. I think he called me a silly bitch. So now, I do not want to get married again because I was seeing another side of him.

Needless to say, the marriage was off for me. My mind went back to the night at my apartment when he invited himself to stay overnight, having jumped into my bed naked. Maybe that was an ego thing, but his behavior now was the same. I was crying and refusing to enter the chapel.

He was screaming and cursing. "You are going to marry me!"

I was too scared to say no. That was a day of living hell. I did not want to get married, but I went through with the ceremony because I was afraid he was going to do something terrible to me, right then or later.

When we went inside Yerkes, JJ wanted to take video pictures and all that. I did not want to have any pictures taken because I had been crying and my eyes were red, my face was twisted, and my hair looked a wreck. The minister said to me, "You don't look too happy, you don't seem to be happy, you don't seem like you want to do this." I wanted to tell him I didn't, but JJ and I got married.

When we left, he started hollering and screaming again, "Why didn't you act happy? What's wrong with you? Why are you acting like this?"

Then he began trying to hug and caress me, saying, "We're married with licenses from the courts. We got on weddings rings. I love you, I love you!"

It could be that I went along with JJ's madness because of his lovemaking. You would have thought he was my old man and I was his young girl. And he was just twenty-six years old, an old soul who knew there was love he could bring out from inside me—and who knew just how to do that. Loving JJ and

JJ loving me made us both fully happy. He had all of me—the beautiful, the ugly, the scared, and the bold. When we made love, we were enjoying some other world no one else knew about.

We were also great together selling Aginah's Herbal Hair Products. I was already doing hair shows in Atlanta and the Bahamas. My hair products could be sold everywhere. I taught JJ how to deliver and sell the products. He started out delivering. Then he sold. He was a great salesmen.

But then he started complaining. "Oh, this is too slow, this money is too slow. You know, I don't know how long I can do this."

Of course I protested. I saw a profitable future for him and for my business with him as our sales representative.

One day he told me he had to leave town for a couple of days.

"Leave town? To go where?"

"I'm going on the road. I've got to go on the road for some friends of mine that own stores in Philadelphia on Jewelers' Row."

I was thinking that he had some kind of legit job he had to do. He left and two days later he called from Las Vegas.

"I'm coming home early; book me a flight for tonight."

I called him back. No flights were leaving Vegas until the next morning. He arrived in Philadelphia early morning, and I picked him up at the airport. He drove to Jewelers' Row to meet his business friends, his "partners" he called them. They gave him lots of money in crispy hundred dollar bills. We drove home. He counted his money and put it into a shoebox. He then asked me to count it over because, he said, his mind didn't stay focused long enough to ensure an accurate count.

I asked him what was going on. I was suspicious.

Then he started talking. "I'm a cat burglar. I'm not a snatch-and-grab boy. The jewelers give me master keys, and I can go anywhere to open jewelry store cases. I go from city to city, state to state, and I go to malls and all kinds of exclusive jewelry stores. I work with a team. We dress up in suits and ties and distract the salespeople so we can unlock the cases with the master keys or take the store keys and take a whole jewelry tray. We bring what we get to my jewelry store partners who pay straight-up cash."

I was thinking that he should have said, "I'm a jewelry thief."

Sometimes his "partners" gave him orders for diamonds of a certain quality or with a particular name. Sometimes they would give him a ring size. He took the master keys and filled the order.

I was saying to myself, *oh my god; I can't live like this. I work too hard to live in discomfort because he's a thief.*

He would come home and have all kinds of diamonds and give me this and give me that. One day he came in after being gone for five days.

"Oh, I have something for you."

He put a diamond tennis necklace around my neck, and I mean it was gorgeous, simply gorgeous.

"You see the tag on here? This tennis necklace cost $30,000."

My facial expression changed.

"You should be grateful, you should be happy," he said. "You didn't say thank you yet, you haven't said anything."

Then came the abuse. He started snapping out on me, "You bitch, you ungrateful bitch."

"I said thank you."

Later that night I told him what was on my mind. "You know it wasn't that I am ungrateful and I didn't want to say thank you. But I don't like the way you got it."

I told him I worked hard. I have calluses on my fingers because I work from sunup to sundown to buy anything and everything I wanted or had. I was fearful his being pulled over while he was driving my brand new white 1994 740 BMW. He would go to jail because of his stealing, and I would go to jail for being in his company.

"All I can see is my name across the front page of the Tribune, 'Aginah Shabazz Caught Stealing,' or Aginah Shabazz caught up in some kind of jewelry ring, whatever, and I don't want that because I'm an honest person."

He said, "Oh, shut the fuck up."

I thought to myself, *Okay, that's what you get, Aginah, for being so stupid. You knew that something was wrong with this boy and you continued to hang on to him.*

Looking back, I don't think I was hanging on solely because of love or whatever. I think I was afraid to leave him, thinking he would really hurt me because he was really madly in love, and I was the first person he had ever married, something he mentioned often. I had to figure out a strategy for getting away from somebody who's crazy.

He continued to do his thing. I hardly spoke to him. I didn't cook. I didn't do anything. I rolled my eyes and sucked my teeth if he asked me to do something—and that was usually to have sex with him, which I started hating because I was always angry and bitter. He would force me to have sex with him.

And that was as unpleasant as it was pleasurable. JJ was totally uninhibited, and he broke down my inhibitions. He was a charming romantic who could be just as nice as he could be nasty. A real live Dr. Jekyll/Mr. Hyde, and that's no joke. People would say, "He's crazy" and I would say, "Yeah, and I don't mean like a fox; he's seriously crazy. Something is really wrong with him." He needs medication.

One day he grabbed a belt and started hitting me with it on my behind. I hadn't provoked him. He was being the werewolf he often became.

"I'm going to beat your ass."

I don't think it was JJ's intention that the belt buckle hit me, but somehow it began to strike my legs and ankles.

"You're hitting me with the buckle." I was screaming and hollering, "You're hitting me with the belt buckle." When he stopped, I was in so much pain that I could hardly move. I was so messed up mentally that I couldn't look at where I had bruises. I moaned and cried while lying in bed and he held me like I was a baby and licked my tears.

"Oh, I'm so sorry, I didn't mean it. I love you so much."

I went to Lankenau Hospital. I got pills to calm my nerves, but I wouldn't reveal that I had been abused. One of the bruises became a lump that stayed on my leg for two years. A girlfriend suggested it was a blood clot.

That incident brought me to my senses. I said to Troy, "You know, I think it would be best that you just leave. I brought some boxes back to pack your things up." He slapped me so hard, I fell to the floor; and when I came to, I was thinking that I couldn't say anything, couldn't do anything—trapped.

On another day, for an entire day, he was throwing one of his insane tantrums. I was a miserable wreck. My son Sultan came home. When my son came in the front door, JJ shut and locked the bedroom door and continued cursing and hollering.

My son knocked on the door, demanding that JJ open the door.

"No, this is my wife. I can say anything I want to her." Minutes later, my son's fist broke through the door.

"No, you're not going to say anything you want to my mother. My mother is all I have. You mean to tell me we let you come here to live with us in our Muslim home and you curse at her like that? My mother doesn't deserve that."

Their voices were getting loud, so I came between them so there wouldn't be a fight.

Sultan ran out. "I'll be back and I'm going to shoot you."

JJ made a phone call and told somebody he was coming to get his gat. I guessed that a gat meant gun. I called my dad and told him to head Sultan off, that he was heading towards Fifty-Ninth Street and to head him off because he was angry and was probably looking for a gun. A short time later my dad called and said that he had Sultan with him. That did it for me. Or at least it should have. I was living in fear of JJ.

He was planning to visit a friend in New York and asked if I would go along. I did not want to go, but I did not want him throwing a tantrum. So I went. We stopped in Manhattan to eat. Then he wanted to shop at Sak's Fifth Avenue.

When we were on the escalator, he said, "Let's stop on third so you can try on the furs."

I said, "I don't need or want a fur coat."

To keep the peace, I went with him to the fur department. He was trying to steal a coat and asked me to try on the coat. Try on a coat? Instead, I walked directly over to the escalator so whoever was watching him would know I am not involved. He came towards me cursing and saying that I left him hanging. I convinced him to leave the store. But when we reached the first floor, he went to the accessory department and began looking at belts.

I said, "I'll wait for you at the entrance and don't steal those people's stuff."

Well, he did. When he got to the entrance, the security guards threw him to floor and put handcuffs on him. They searched him. He had three alligator skin belts—he had to steal something. I began walking around asking the store clerks how to get to the security office, but no one knew—or pretended not to know.

I stood in the lobby of the main entrance waiting to learn the outcome. Around 8:00 p.m., a woman came to ask me if she could search me. An expensive dress was missing from the woman's department.

"Sure you can," I said. "And when you don't find anything on me, I will sue and own shares in Sak's Fifth Avenue."

She looked unsure. She did not search me. I learned JJ had been arrested for petty larceny. I asked if she could get my car keys and parking ticket from JJ so I could go home. About a half hour later, a store detective approached me. He asked if I knew the name of the guy they had just arrested.

"You mean he didn't give you his name?"

"Yes, he did, but we think it's an alias."

"I really don't know much about him. We just met a few weeks ago. When he asked me out on a date I didn't know we were coming to New York for dinner. I guess he wanted to surprise me? His name is Joseph."

"Joseph what?"

"I don't know, whatever he told you.

He said, "You are as stupid as they come."

"Yes, I am," I replied. "Sir, I need to drive back to Philly, and Joseph has the parking ticket in his pocket."

"If you tell me his last name, I will give you the ticket."

I wanted to tell him JJ's last name so I could leave the cold hallway and go home, but I was afraid to tell because it may not have been the name he had given them. So I had to wait another hour before he finally bought me the ticket and the keys. As he gave them to me, the police were bringing JJ out in handcuffs. I asked the officer what station he was taking him. He told me, and I drove to the police station, pretending to be concerned. Maybe I was.

I was mostly concerned about getting back to Philly. It was after midnight. I was trying to thaw out from freezing in that hallway. I was tired and dozing off during the drive home. I thanked God for getting me home safe. I was so disgusted that I couldn't think straight, but I was hoping it was the end of our marriage. I believe that thought kept me awake long enough to drive the one hundred miles home. When I reached my bedroom, I struggled to get undressed, threw my clothes on the floor, and hopped in bed without showering or anything.

Would you believe that JJ called me the next day to ask why I left New York? He said I should have stayed overnight in a hotel. I thought *that's what wives do when they don't care if their husbands get caught stealing while in their company*. I felt violated.

He was convicted of a misdemeanor, did eight hours of community service, and caught a train home. A couple of weeks later, his probation officer and the police came to arrest him. He called me from jail, and I told him, "Don't ever call me ever again in life."

"The parole officer said you sent me here. You sent me here. I'm going to kill you."

I got a letter from JJ. It contained a picture of a body on a coroner's stretcher. The face on the body was mine. He had cut it from a photograph. His note said: "This is you because I'm going to kill you when I get out of here because I really believe you put me here."

While he was in prison, I informed him I wanted a divorce. He said he wanted to discuss it in person. I should visit him, bringing the paperwork. I simply needed to give it to the visiting room officer.

When I arrived at the state penitentiary at Gratersford, the guard told me I had to mail the papers or pay a sheriff to deliver them to him. I went downstairs to the visiting room. He was so excited; he hugged me like he missed me. Then he flipped into the werewolf, cursing me, calling me all kinds of names. There must have been fifty people in that visiting room. I was humiliated and embarrassed, but more than anything I was afraid he would hit me.

I sat there saying to myself, *How are you going to get your stupid ass out of here before this nut slaps you hard enough to hurt you so bad you'll need to be carried out on a stretcher?*

I was looking at the exit out of the corner of my eye trying to position where each guard stood or sat. Some sat up high in a booth right in front of me and there was one at the exit. The guard that was walking around was walking in my direction, and when he walked back around that was my cue. When he was right in front of me, I quickly jumped up and hightailed it over to the exit door.

"Officer, please let me out. Open the door. I've got to leave."

"Well, are you all right?"

"No! That's a crazy man in there and I've got to get away from him."

I turned around and looked at JJ. Would you believe he was standing there begging, "Please don't leave me, don't leave, oh, Aginah, don't leave, don't leave."

I turned and said, "You stupid motherfucker." I called him all the names he called me. I got a great kick out of cursing him—and so did the guards. I ran up the steps. The female guard at the top of the stairs said to me, "Well, that was quick."

"Yeah, I wasn't going to be anyone's stupid bitch and dumb hoe. That was my last time."

"Hum, you need to tell that to a whole lot of those women down there because those girls are humiliated every day and keep coming back."

"Well, you won't see me back here ever again" and I left. I felt relief that words cannot express.

By the time I arrived home, JJ was on the phone begging and crying. I changed my telephone number. I sent him a letter informing him I had started divorce proceedings.

"I've tried to come to some kind of agreement with you and tried to enter into a peaceful divorce, but you showed me you, the Werewolf, in living color. My final decision is you'll never have to worry about me anymore in life."

I handled the divorce myself. An attorney friend told me to go to a stationery store for the forms. I gave him a set, and he filled in everything I needed to say. I typed what I needed to type and then took the forms to the Montgomery County Courthouse for filing.

The clerk asked, "Are you going to serve him or do you want us to?"

"Oh no, I'm going to pay the sheriff to serve him." I think I paid the sheriff eighty dollars or something like that. Whatever, I paid the fee. I was notified when he was served.

His mother called me weeks later. "You served JJ with divorce papers?"

"Yes, I did."

"Well, I'm glad because I never thought you two were supposed to be married anyway. Not because I didn't like you—you were the best thing for him—but my son has problems. I was trying to tell you in a roundabout way because I knew if he did something to you that you would retaliate by having something done to him. And I didn't want that to happen to my son."

She didn't want anything to happen to her son. Okay, fine. And I didn't want anything to happen to me.

After I heard from the Montgomery County Courthouse that the divorce papers were served and accepted by him, I had an "exhale" party while waiting for my decree. My girlfriend, Yolanda, dubbed me a tape to play, all the Waiting to Exhale songs. All my friends came to the dinner party. We had a wonderful time. I enjoyed myself as repayment for all the months I had lived in misery married to JJ.

It was the joke of the night—exhale party, yes! I felt like I had just delivered a fifteen-pound baby. My insides were now relaxed and relieved of so much pain, so much fear and negative energy.

When I received my divorce decree, I literally INHALED and EXHALED. It was all over! But it was not really all over because I hadn't changed the salon's telephone number yet. JJ was still calling and threatening me. He had hooked up with a girl who had been visiting somebody else in the prison. In fact, she used to live with his brother. She started visiting him. And then she started calling.

"What are you calling for?"

"I'm calling because he wants his stuff."

"What stuff—what are you talking about?"

Then he called. He tried to blackmail me with pictures of me half nude he had taken when we were married. He had them in prison with him and was threatening to send them out to all of the hair salons. At first, I was a little paranoid. But then, one day I said to him, "Send them. In fact, send them to Playboy. Maybe Playboy will accept them and I'll make millions and send you a few dollars to put on your commissary book."

He stopped threatening me with the pictures and mailed them back to me.

Then JJ asked for everything he had given me, even my wedding dowry. I went to see my grandmother before she passed away to talk about what I was going through. She knew before I said anything.

"You don't look good these days. Something is bothering you. What has you looking and feeling so miserable?"

Grandmother Leslie is very spiritual and clairvoyant. She reads you easily. My presence suggested to her that something was wrong, and the look on my face confirmed it. Before I could say anything, she said, "He is a terrible acting person who does not deserve to be loved by a woman as wonderful as you."

"Grandmom, JJ is an Indian giver and wants all his material things returned to him."

"Give him all his things. You just said some of them were stolen things? Give him everything that he has ever given you, even the things he paid for, all the way down to the antique knickknacks."

I did exactly that. I came home, called JJ's grandmother and told her I was bringing everything to her. JJ told her to put the things in storage. I drove

Ms. Betty to the storage place and removed JJ's things from my car. Whatever jewelry was left, I gave to her. There were three fur coats, antique vases, and candelabra pieces that I really wanted to keep, but I gave them back because they were stolen. There was also an exquisite Erte statue that set in my living room on a pedestal. In 1994, that statue cost eight thousand dollars when he stole it. Today the price has tripled. I gave that back too. I gave everything back.

He called the salon one day to ask if I had given him back everything.

"I took it all to the storage bin. As for a few pieces of jewelry, your grandmother has them, and what she doesn't have is in the pawnshop."

"Pawnshop?"

"Yes, did you really think I was giving you back all my jewelry without collecting some money for it? After all, you still owe me for three-thousand dollars in prison collect calls."

In the next breath, he had the nerve to say that by asking me to return everything; he was only trying to bribe me into loving him again.

"Why else would I ask you to give me all my stuff back?" he argued.

I just hung up the phone—click. I thought to myself that my life has certainly been a mess because of choices I made. It seemed like after I removed all that stolen merchandise from my house, just as my grandmother had predicted, a halo of light came over my home. I thanked God for that calm and peace I began to feel.

Light had replaced darkness. It was bright and clear. I thought angels had been present and recorded what good I had done. No more stolen goods and I felt good. I felt damn good until JJ's new girlfriend started calling the hair salon.

"I'm going to cut you-like cut me with a knife. I'm going to come there to cut you from A to Z," she said. I thought Dumb and Dumber. At the time, my sister was there. My sister, Sheila, agreed to answer the phone the next time she called.

She said, "Yeah, come on. We're waiting for you."

"Well, who is this?" the caller said.

"This is Aginah's sister, and I'm going to wait for you so you better hurry up, bitch."

Of course, she never appeared. I left work early and went home. My head was hurting, and I was feeling sick to my stomach. My nerves were a wreck. JJ and the girlfriend having my number was a problem. I could not change the number because it the salon's number. I had to figure out something.

One of my clients was a state representative. I went to her house to show her the picture of me JJ glued to paper on an ambulance stretcher. She said, "Oh, I thought he was such a nice guy, and I remember we were all saying Aginah has a nice young husband, very handsome. Then we find out he's verbally and physically abusive."

She contacted the commissioner of prisons. JJ spent six months in solitary confinement because of the threats and the phone calls. When his girlfriend called me, I was told to report calls from his girlfriend. I did, and he was punished for that too. Whenever he came up for parole, he was denied. He was given the explanation that it was feared he would attack me, something, for which the state would be held responsible. He had to do his maximum time.

Years later, he wrote and asked me to go back to the state representative and rescind my complaint. I don't think that option was available to me, but I wasn't going to try, and I told him. He was upset, and he also said things like: "People make mistakes; she understands that I was crazy in love with you and just talking crazy because you left me in jail."

I let him max out his time. Every time he came up for parole, I would get a letter informing me he had been denied. I was informed when JJ was released and given the name of a detective to contact if he came anywhere near me.

One day I was at Delilah's restaurant, Bluezette's, having dinner with Stephanie, Valerie, and Sheila. JJ was there. He walked over to our booth, spoke to everybody, and invited himself to sit with us. He asked about seeing me alone.

"How have you been? I'm checking up on you because you know you're still my wife. What have you been doing?"

I said nothing.

"I hear you're going away? It's your birthday soon and your time to go to the Bahamas, huh?"

"Yes. I leave in two days."

"Can I get your cell number?"

That Friday, he called me. "Can you meet me at Friday's?"

"For what?"

"I've got a birthday gift for you to take to the Bahamas with you."

I met him, and he gave me a thousand dollars. I thanked him. He introduced me to the girl who was with him. I left and went home. I left the next day for my vacation.

JJ used to call occasionally. We would talk and laugh.

"Wow, we're the best of friends."

"Yes."

I didn't want to be his wife anymore. I didn't want to be his girlfriend either, and I really didn't want to go out with him—though I had love for him. And he had love for me.

JJ was a man with whom I fell in love. And the love relationship became a love-hate relationship. I loved him as much as I hated him. It was something out of a novel. As I close this chapter, I realize that JJ and I were very much the same but completely different. We were meant to come together to save each other.

Of all my relationships, I think I learned the most from JJ about my womanhood. I learned how easily it was for a happy woman to become an unhappy woman. JJ was much younger than me, but because of my insecurities, I fell for him. He made me happy. He made me sad. He made me excited. He could lift my spirits and drag me through the mud.

A woman should not allow a man to have such power over her. I learned that neither JJ nor anyone else could make me happy—that they could only add to my happiness. To be happy and be comfortable in my own skin with or without JJ had been my choice to make. I did make that choice, and maybe I could have made it sooner. Nonetheless, I learned the lesson and then made the right choice.

If I may, let me brief you about JJ, the young man I married in August 1994. Following are excerpts from an article that I got online after I divorced JJ. Believe it or not, he is very proud of the article.

The excerpts are rendered from the actual article but the names have changed.

TROUBLE MORE WAYS THAN YOU CAN NAME JUVENILE AUTHORITIES HAD THEIR HANDS FULL WITH JJ MAYBE THAT'S WHY HE KEPT SLIPPING THROUGH THEIR FINGERS

To appreciate JJ's travels through the city's juvenile justice system, consider the numbers:

He was arrested under at least 32 names, 21 different addresses—some of them vacant lots—and 13 dates of birth.

The pint-sized crime prodigy entered the city's juvenile system early and often. Four days after his 10th birthday, in May 1978, he stole $20 from a nun standing on a Southwest Philadelphia street corner. He skipped his court date, but was arrested twice more within a month for another pickpocket incident and a purse snatch.

At 12 he stole his first car, a maroon Cadillac. Barely big enough to see over the steering wheel, JJ managed to get the car from Ocean City to Philadelphia, where he was arrested after a hit and run. He ran away from home the next day, stealing $80 from an uncle.

During the 18 months he spent at a wilderness school and foster home in western Pennsylvania, JJ, then 14, ran away at least four times—stealing two cars and a van.

By the time he was 16 he had turned pro, working the parking lots of Philadelphia and Ocean City for a stolen car ring. He specialized in Mercedes-Benzes.

His crimes touched the lives of at least 118 victims and witnesses from all walks of life: the 78-year-old woman knocked to the street for her purse; the cabbie involuntarily parted from $150 in fare money and a personal check; the woman wrestled to the sidewalk inside City Hall courtyard; the Main Line doctor and the wife of a prominent lawyer who lost their new, $24,000-plus Mercedes.

"The system failed," said N. Jackson, chief of the Defenders Association's juvenile unit. "The person who lost here was JJ. But we all lose because JJ is costing us."

Jackson remembers JJ, whom he started representing in 1979, as "the most petite, cute little guy you could lay your eyes on." His diminutive appearance and traumatic history—he watched his mother's boyfriend shoot and paralyze her when he was 4—made people "bend over backward" to help him.

But JJ was exceptionally bright and manipulative, according to Jackson: "He outsmarted the system."

The JJ case "points out the need for changes in the law to allow us to fingerprint and photograph juveniles," Deputy DA Brown said. "It's a hole in the system that people take advantage of. The new legislation would help prevent that.

Such laws could have helped catch up with JJ be fore he became a one-boy crime wave, prosecutors and police believe.

They knew JJ as a street-smart youth who led a small band of younger kids from the Diamond Street Homes public housing project. The kids specialized in stealing luxury cars and strong-arming elderly people as they exited banks with items retrieved from safety deposit boxes.

By the time he was 14, JJ had been placed in group homes, foster homes, reform schools, mental health facilities, a wilderness camp. He ran away from them all. Finally, in 1983, he spent about six months in the secure unit of the juvenile detention center in Cornwells Heights, Bucks County.

According to records, JJ reads at a first-grade level. He witnessed his mother's shooting at age 7, and claimed his father was a Black Mafia member who had been shot to death. His mother, who now uses a walker, was confined to a wheelchair when JJ was young and was unable to care for him. He lived with relatives, friends or in the streets.

One psychiatrist who evaluated JJ when he was 11 noted, "He shows a world-weary look, old and streetwise beyond his tender years."

Jackson, of the Defenders Association, said JJ's family history, his small size and his youth had initially convinced judges and probation officers to treat him as a dependent or deprived child rather than a delinquent.

The records indicate JJ's family situation didn't help matters. When he was sent to a foster home in Pittsburgh, for example, he ran away after his mother sent him money to come home. Later, police charged two of JJ's female relatives with signing him out of police custody under false names.

Even as an adult convicted in the four stolen car cases, JJ spent little time in jail. The judge who sentenced him to 11 1/2 to 23 months could not by law take his lengthy juvenile record into account.

"I'm sure he thinks the adult system is also a terrible joke," former prosecutor McQueen said. Now, no one in the system can say where JJ is.

"His record dictates the first place we should look for him is prison," Detective Lewis said. "He could be your next-door neighbor living under an assumed name. He could be the reverend around the corner . . . He could be driving away in your new car."

Chapter Thirteen

Justice for Her

Aginah

The impact of prison was hard and instant. In the brief time it takes to respond to a doorbell, Nas lost her freedom, her family, and any hope of a future. Over and over again she would ask herself how she got to such a place. Was it all her fault? Was she guilty or had she been deceived? Was her imprisonment just or unjust?

Nas

Every day I was in prison, I thought about how many women were in here because of some man. How many women had children and families waiting for them to come home? The hardest pill to swallow was how many women weren't leaving here because they had a life sentence in jail because of some mistake they made on their own or by becoming an accomplice to a man's illegal activities and because some man convinced her he loved her and she *fell* hard for him.

The only difference between them and me was that my cry for justice was carried out largely by my mother, sending a shock wave through my family, the community, and ultimately through the halls of the criminal justice system.

Illegal drugs have devastated the black community. You can drive through the ghetto on any given day and see people sitting on steps and hanging on corners selling drugs. Although most of the media attention is paid to the dealers who are mostly men, drug dealing has had a devastating effect on black women. There are women going to prison. There are the newspaper headlines about women and children getting caught in gun-battle cross fires.

Drug dealing is a by-product of a disfranchised people's desire to live the "American dream." The media plays a role in promoting greed and glorifying crime as a way to get money. The media portrays the gangsters, black mafia and Italian mafia, with sensationalism. When it comes to understanding major trends in any community such as the drug-dealing trend in urban areas, you have to look at history and the larger society to find answers. You can't just blame victims. You have to look at the injustices. But it's also important to look at family and personal responsibility.

Aginah

Because my daughter was charged with conspiracy to murder a known drug dealer, she faced the death penalty. This ripped my heart out. My entire family, especially her three children, was devastated. I kept asking myself why something like this happened to us. Is guilt by association truth in America? Was Nas's mistake the company she kept? Was her crime her longing for the wrong things from the wrong people?

For my daughter, life in the Philadelphia community used to be simple, even predictable. But Nas fell victim to a government conspiracy that entailed wiretaps and entrapment, all leading to her unjustified arrest as a prime suspect in a capital crime investigation.

My determination to fight for my daughter's life and bring justice to an unjust situation took us all on a twisted journey into a world of lies, deceit, manipulation, and government fraud and courtroom drama.

My persistence and power of love brought everyone together—family, extended family, friends, clients, and employees—against the judicial system to prove my daughter's innocence. Why did the government set up Nas? Was the capture of a so-called "drug kingpin" so important that the innocent lives of a mother and her children should be sacrificed in order to make the case for the premier assistant district attorney? You will discover the horrifying truth when I reveal the ultimate setup.

DA Roger King, also a black man, had waited a long time to get revenge for Darryl winning a retrial. The lies he told were what he thought were needed to get Nas to testify against Darryl.

During the thirty-day intensive and dramatic court proceedings, the court stenographer recorded lie after lie. This was a living nightmare for this victim of acquaintance whose only indiscretion was her choice of men. She could not believe that an error in judgment so long ago would have consequences of this magnitude.

Bail was denied twice because the prosecutor lied about having wiretaps implicating Nas in organized crime. He accused Yonzetta of being an assassin and a flight risk. She was humiliated, railroaded, and stressed to the point of collapse. She was separated from her beloved children for a heartbreaking eighteen months.

Nas's daughter, Aginah E, nine years old at the time, asked if she could speak with the judge presiding over her mother's bail hearing. It was hard for her, but the words just rolled off her tongue as if she had rehearsed her speech. She explained to the judge what a good mother she had and how hard it was to not have her mother in her life. She talked about their sleepovers and the fact that now her bed was empty. She begged the judge to give her mother bail. While clearly moved by her pleas, the judge was bound by law to deny bail given the "evidence" that had been presented to her.

We lost the chance to bring Nas home. We lost! I kept hearing the bad news echoing in my head. I was crying hysterically. I was limp and motionless. There was nothing anyone could say to comfort me. I thought to myself that maybe if I had not ignored the voices inside me telling me to keep my defenses up, I wouldn't be feeling so much pain. Pain was in my head, my face, my stomach, my hands, and my feet.

The only thing left for me to do at that moment was grab hold of my granddaughter's hand and rush home to pray. I sobbed quietly then loudly and prayed softly and out loud. My heart, body, and spirit now stood defiant and in opposition to what the court said about the case. The battle had just begun—Nas was coming home—God willing.

Now, I was forced to become the mother, not just the grandmother, of Nas's three children. The children had to move in with me. I had a spare room that had been my son's, and I brought them from their home in Germantown to my two-bedroom condo. Everyone was crowded in but loved. The boys were still going to a Philadelphia school in Roxborough, and Aginah went to Fitler, an academic school. I drove back and forth across the city driving my grandchildren to school every morning until I enrolled them in the Lower Merion school district where I lived.

I lived alone for many years. It dawned on me that my lifestyle was changing overnight. What am I going to cook for dinner? What about breakfast? I was overwhelmed. I had to cook and clean because I couldn't afford Ms. Genny the housekeeper anymore. I was also helping three children with homework and doing the laundry. And, believe me, that homework was not fun for me. I remember calling the school to ask a teacher if she could send me the answers. I couldn't sign the homework if the answers were wrong.

All of this was going on, and I still had to go to work, visit Nas in prison, and manage things at the salon. These were children who needed all the love and attention they could get. I wanted to give them everything they wanted and needed because their mother could not be there for them.

It was difficult to deal with suburban schools that had a very small black population. I found myself fighting with the Lower Merion school district while fighting for my daughter's life in the criminal justice system. Bala-cynwyd Middle School tried to label Nas's middle child, Eric, as learning disabled. I requested independent testing outside the Lower Merion school district. A psychologist, Dr. Richard Hess, found test score results in the high to superior range for Eric. Believe it or not, the administrators at the Bala-cynwyd Middle School blatantly ignored Dr. Hess's evaluation and transferred Eric without my permission to Welsh Valley Middle School, another suburban school, one that offered a program called "Pride," a learning support program they said he needed.

Eric expressed frustration with the level of work and requested more challenging opportunities, which he did not get. Because of the stigma attached to the PRIDE program, Eric felt ostracized from the regular education students. His self-esteem and confidence began to diminish. I attribute that partly to racist white folks using their superiority to break 'em down, "break the spirit" of black boys—which was done to black males during slavery.

Mothers and grandmothers do not grow weary of advocating for your children. They are being sent through the pipeline—from the schools to the prisons. At this writing, Lower Merion school district is being sued by the Mainline branch of Concerned Black Parents and the NAACP. Eric is one of the plaintiffs.

While in the struggle for my daughter there were still good things happening in my life. My son, Sultan, enrolled at Cheyney University in 1998, the same year his sister was arrested. I was torn financially between supporting my son and supporting my daughter. Without a doubt, he deserved my financial support one hundred percent. I spent many restless nights thinking about how I could support both causes at the same time. Where was I going to get the money for a lawyer and pay college tuition? I called my niece Aminah Shabazz, who was majoring in accounting at the school, to ask if she knew of a way that my son could apply for grants and loans to pay for his first semester. She had the answer, and she helped him fill out applications. Tuition was paid.

Nas

Jail life for me was extremely difficult. Upon entering prison, I was issued a number in place of my name. Then I was stripped-searched, forced to take off all my clothes in front of the guards. Made to take a shower, the guard simply stood there. I asked, "Are you going to just stand there and watch me?" She responded, "Yeah, I have to watch you!" That's when I broke down and started crying. I felt so degraded.

Then I was taken to a cell. I looked for a bed. What I saw was a thin mat, like a mat that you would flip on in a gym. The cell was nasty and dirty. I looked for a window to open in order to get a little fresh air. There were windows but they didn't open. My first thought was *This ain't no window. Windows open.* This was just a square with bars, something used to simply let sunshine in. The food smelled bad. On my first day in the prison chow hall, other inmates commented.

"Girl, you better eat that food!"

"I don't eat no dark meat. And that chicken ain't even done!"

"Well, ain't you gonna eat your bread?"

"I don't eat no white bread!"

"Where you think you at?"

"Anyway, I don't plan on being here that long. I'll be out in three to ten days!"

Jail wasn't easy for me. In order to cope, I started working in the prison beauty salon, but the cigarette smoke affected my asthma condition. I switched to the laundry room.

The prison laundry was a huge room filled with large, industrial-sized washing machines and dryers. One day while on a visit with my mom, she asked, "What are those burn marks up and down your arms, what are they from?" The laundry room was extremely hot. Those huge machines give off a tremendous amount of heat. The only clothing worn in prison are orange jumpsuits. These are washed by the hundreds in the laundry. The jumpsuits have small metal snaps. The snaps heat up and cause severe burns when you take them out of the hot dryer to fold.

I worked so many hours that I would be totally exhausted by the end of the day. But the job gave me an escape from my misery and a means by which to pass the time away. I could also think about all the bad choices I made.

Actual letter to Trial Judge

The Honorable James A. Lineberger
1404 Criminal Justice Center
1301 Filbert Street
Philadelphia, PA. 19107

Dear Judge Lineberger,

I am the mother of Yonzetta Hudson, who has been held in the custody of the Commonwealth of Pennsylvania since April of 1998, under the file number 80181 CP No. 9805-0657. I can honestly tell you that I have not known a moment's peace since that dreadful moment. In the seventeen months that have passed, I have prayed unceasingly that God, in His infinite mercy, would move the legal wheels along with all deliberate speed and put an end to this painful experience that has kept my daughter incarcerated for so long. It is with this in mind that I am writing to you, hoping that I can communicate my concerns, Not just as the parent of the accused, but as the grandparent of her children.

Yonzetta was scheduled to go to trial on June 14, 1999, but because her co-defendant's lawyer withdrew from the case, due to an inability to be paid for services, a court appointed attorney had to be assigned, and as a result, the proceedings were postponed to October 4, 1999, until the new attorney could become adequately prepared to represent his client. I am very worried about the prospect of this case being dragged out for an additional length of time, causing stress in the extreme on Yonzetta who has no involvement with this attorney, and her three children, who have suffered terribly in their mother's absence.

I realize the momentum of the case as it heads toward trial is not mine to establish; however, Yonzetta's attorney has been ready to go forth in her defense since the original trial date was set. I know the damage that has already been done because of the delay, especially to Yonzetta's family. I see the distress in her children's lives every day, as I am the one who is caring for them. Thus, it is my fervent wish, if the trial undergoes another delay, that you consider placing Yonzetta under house arrest, with work privileges. Such arrangement would permit having begun at a young age working with me, building a cosmetology business in several locations around Philadelphia. Even a strict house arrest would suffice, if work privileges are not allowable, because her children would have the benefit of her presence. They could regain some sense of stability, while the attorneys for the co-defendant make themselves ready.

Your honor, I am an up-standing, contributing member of society. I've owned and operated a hair salon for twenty-one years. I tried very hard to instill strong values in my children. I know Yonzetta's character, as do many people throughout Philadelphia. I feel confident, that at some point in the trial, who Yonzetta really is will be known to all and she will be exonerated of all charges. In the meantime, I am asking for grace, a chance to restore the family, in the event things do not go as planned.

Most respectfully,
Aginah Shabazz

Chapter Fourteen

Grandmom Leslie

Her word was the whole truth. And it was nothing but the truth—so help her God. Leslie Banks-Glenn stood at the center of her family, radiating power.

She had Native American features with cream-colored smooth skin. Her hair was white and wavy, reaching almost to her waist. But she always styled her hair pulled back from her face into a bun. Grandmom Leslie was a big woman, literally and figuratively, weighing well over two hundred fifty pounds. She dominated her children and grandchildren with a mighty will, and she had the devotion of them all.

The younger of her two daughters and the first to get married and own a home was my mother, Elizabeth. No matter where my mother lived, she would always be drawn back to her mother. Always wanting to feel secure in her mother's love, Elizabeth moved her mother into her home wherever we moved. She raised her children to believe in God and to appreciate that being poor was not a handicap. Though her four children did not dress in expensive clothing, they were clean. They did not graduate high school or attended colleges but they were intelligent. They had faith, a loving home, good morals, good manners and she taught them how to respect everyone.

My grandfather would leave her alone with no money to pay bills. He would leave for work washing windows—he was a window washer. Grandmom tried to hold herself together until she could no longer sit home alone without any money for food and bills. When times became too hard to resist, grandmom would head down to the neighborhoods where he worked. She didn't drive so my mother would gather up her children and would drive around in search of her dad. I remember as a little girl feeling Grandmom Leslie's pain while she searched for her husband.

My grandfather was a window washer. And he was an alcoholic whose preference was cheap wine. He would get paid and get drunk. I recall as a little girl riding with my mother and grandmom Leslie, my mother driving, searching "skid row" for him. She would usually find him, drunk and asleep on somebody's steps. Grandmom's subtle rage would turn to tears. Grandpop would return home with new promises and hopes, but he was an alcoholic, and in those days, there were no programs for people with addictions or diseases. Through all of the heartache, Grandmom Leslie was strong and a survivor.

I remember "Grandmom Leslie" building a home-based business. She crocheted scarves and doilies for people for a small fee. She also made money hand washing and ironing the handmade scarves whenever her customers would return. She was known as someone who could make fancy tablecloths in a short time. Even when she lived with us, she continued to crochet for family and friends. She also did all the cooking and cleaning. I loved being around her and I always had plenty of questions to ask.

"Can you show me how to do that, grandmom?" I asked.

"What are you doing that for, grandmom?"

"Why do I have to thread your sewing needle, grandmom?"

"You eyes will know one day when you get to be my age," she said.

"Why can't you iron that lady's doilies without first soaking them in that blue liquid starch?"

"They will not stand out, plus anything you do for people do it the best you can no matter how much money they pay you."

"Grandmom, why are we putting cooked sweet potatoes inside this white cloth?"

"Cheesecloth." She'd say, "We squeezing the strings out, strings wrap around your intestines and could strangle them."

Grandmom Leslie's energy and perseverance brought her a loving and unforgiving nature.

In my memories of her, she is still large and powerful.

Grandmom Leslie took ill, so I visited her at my mother's home. I sat right by her medical bed.

"Is it too warm in here?" I asked.

"No, it feels fine to me," she said, but I was sweating.

The room is too small and hot to have no air circulating. I sat in the chair closest to her bed and turned on the fan.

On that hot summer day, Grandmom was reading her Bible. I've seen that Bible lying on a dresser beside her bed all my life. It didn't just lie there; she read it every day. Everyone knew her deep belief in God. She knew and memorized many verses and would sometimes read aloud to her grandchildren. She always gave us a verse to remember.

Sitting there with her in my mother's house seemed to have memories echoing back through generations: the physical abuse my mother experienced living there and my painful experiences living in that house too. I was either there to confront the deep knifelike pains that left emotional scars on all of us or I was there to find the strength to confront a new emotional shock—Nas's death penalty case.

I reached into my handbag for the legal documents Grandmom asked me to have a lawyer draft. She wanted me to have the power of attorney should anything happen to her. I knew it would be family drama if I pulled out those papers should anything happened to her. Nonetheless, she signed them and the only two people knew was my sister and me. Now I was responsible for Grandmom in her life and death and that was fine with me, since my sister and our dad had brought her from a nursing home in Harrisburg, Pennsylvania to our mother's house, so she could be surrounded by her family.

I watched as my grandmother's age took a toll on her body. Leslie's eyes were tired. She laid down the Bible, sticking a marker inside to hold her page. I looked into her tired eyes and saw my own reflections, not mirror images but control or discipline, stubbornness which has survived generations passed down from her, my mother, me, and Nas. I also sensed from observing my mother and grandmother our temperaments, our family drama, and our choices that linked us together.

It was getting late and I had to get back home before my three grandchildren arrived home from school. I kissed her before I left.

"I'll see you tomorrow, Grandmom." Actually, I wouldn't see her there anymore—it was the day my aunt Madeline took her to live at the St. Ignatius nursing home in West Philadelphia.

I visited my grandmother at the St. Ignatius nursing home several months before she died. The last time I heard her voice was when I stood beside her one hour before her death. As always, she anticipated my visit with pleasure. Her last words to me were "What took you so long to get here?"

In a whisper, I said, "Grandmom, it's been so painful for me to see you here and to know it will not be long before your departure."

"God is ready for me and I'm ready to go. But I want you to get yourself together to be strong for Nas's kids. Nas is going to be all right." She'll be home soon.

"Okay, Grandmom."

"And don't have the prison guards take her out of prison to attend my funeral; it's nothing but more pain for her—she wants to remember me talking to her in person."

I still miss her.

That day, I got on my knees and made prayer.

After prayer, I put on tan slacks with a tan tunic top and a pair of brown leather ankle boots and a brown leather jacket I got as a gift from my good friend David to wear throughout the trial to keep me warm. I walked up City Line Avenue to take the R5 train so I didn't have to pay for parking and I could think. I probably couldn't drive and think at the same time. I was going through too much.

When I got to the courthouse, I was searched and given a ticket to retrieve my cell phone at the end of the day. As I got to the door of the courtroom, the prosecutor was walking out as I was trying to go in. He never did look at me; he looked down instead. I was hoping that he would look at me. He didn't want to squeeze by me so he motioned to me with his hand to come on in so he could walk on out. I didn't want to move by him; I wanted him to look at me. I wanted him to look me in the eyes but he didn't. He walked out with his head down.

"God has a plan and you have a plan, but God is the best of planners," I said to him. I don't think he heard me, but I wanted to say it anyway because my grandmother had said it to me.

Grandmom Leslie is the ultimate source of comfort in my family. That is so because she so sincerely depends on God. She has true god-conscious. I realize I am speaking about her as though she was alive and she is not. She is someone I can grow to become. She was my source of strength during the trial. She is the one who conveys true wisdom. Her life parallels with mine, my mother's, and that of my daughter's. Her husband the window cleaner symbolizes the almost-but-not-quite men I, Nas, and my mother have dealt with. She said while crocheting that I will learn in time what she has learned over time. She puts her affairs in my hands at the time of her death because I am the God-fearing one. She died knowing justice will prevail. Nas lives as she dies. Nas may turn out to be the true strong woman among the three of us.

Aginah

Aginah, Mary and Stephanie

Aginah & Stylist

David and Nas

Shabazz Family

Fundraiser Committee

Nas Wedding

Sultan II and son Sultan III

Omar, Eric and Little Aginah

Aginah and Nas

Lt. Gerald 3X
Photograph by Rubin Bashir

Nassau, The Bahamas

Sultan, Sheila, and David

Jamal

Aginah and Nas

Grandmom Leslie

Nas and her new baby, Anisa

Aginah

Nas

Chapter Fifteen

JFH Fund-raisers

I pulled a "Dream Team" together to see how I could raise money and hired a Muslim lawyer, Tariq El-Shabazz. I actually did not know what I was up against regarding the money I would need to pay for Nas' bail and attorney fees. But listening to other people I thought I would have to pay a high bail, maybe in the 50,000 dollar bracket and I would need cash money. I estimated, in my head, the combined total cost for lawyer fees and private investigators. The private investigator would have to travel to Detroit to get background information about the two co-defendants. I thought about traveling costs too. I thought maybe it could cost me close to $100,000. This was money I did not have. I reached out to the community for support to raise funds to pay whatever I needed to get my daughter out of jail.

I called Bruce who owned Rivage, a swanky ballroom on East River Drive to ask what it would cost to have fundraisers at his venue. He said I could use his place free of charge. Thank God for Bruce. He said if it were my daughter, he would hope people would do the same for him. Anyway I called a meeting with several of my good friends to meet at Rivage ballroom. I was on a mission and determined to save my daughter. Dr. Rosa Lewis, Stephanie Beyah, Sheila Drakeford, Janice Winston, Cheryl Bullock, Linda Jasper, Salaam Muhsin and Gregory Turner all showed up. Everyone began discussing what they could do. Throughout this meeting, I began to feel I wasn't in this alone. I felt strengthened by my "Dream Team." I was very pleased that I had their fundraising efforts and support. They all worked tirelessly to help save Nas. My family, friends, community, and even people who somehow heard about Nas situation, supported our every decision to raise funds to "FREE NAS."

I decided for our first fundraiser, we would sell tickets for fifty dollars. Of course people complained that no one would pay that much for a dance without a sit down dinner. I heard them but something deep down inside me said, "Make it fifty dollars." Food was donated by Delilah, my friend and a well known restaurateur. We had tickets printed, hired a DJ and confirmed she would prepare food for the buffet. Everyone was given a specific amount of tickets they would be responsible for, and the rest of the tickets were sold at the salon. Brother Fareed Nurridin paid for all the radio Ads for the fundraisers.

Family, friends, clients and people we didn't even know came out in strong support. The ballroom was packed. The young people that didn't come inside hung out in the parking lot after they came inside to buy a ticket. The first fundraiser grossed nine thousand dollars—just a dance and a buffet. My thinking was profitable. I had a goal and a reward followed. So you see I didn't listen to those folk who said it couldn't happen.

I was focused on nothing else but doing hair to make money and raising money for my daughter's case. I was not about to allow the system to swallow her up alive. One of our top stylists, Marquita Oliver, was very supportive of Nas and me. She put her college education on hold to hold down the fort at the salon to continue doing hair sun-up to sun-down making money when my anxiety and depression wouldn't allow me to make it into the salon.

Dr. Rosa opened the bank account, made all the deposits and wrote all the checks. Janice would collect all the money at each event. She was also responsible for meeting with the Lawyer for updates and to pay him. Rosa would cut a check and give it to Janice to pay for all services that would help Nas and her children.

We paid Kareem Shabazz the private investigator to take a plane to Detroit to meet with law enforcers. He told us that he wanted to find out who were the District Attorneys star witness and Nas' co-defendant. The information he came back with was so valuable to the trial. He had to also visit another co-defendant who was doing time in a Pittsburg Correctional Institutional.

A lot was going on, while we sold tickets for the events, we would also sell things in-house. "My Dream Team" again was responsible for their quota of cheesecakes. Yes, we sold cheesecakes in the salon. Donald, my dad was the driver who picked up all the products we bought to raise more money. He also delivered to those who ordered by phone. We planned three additional dances at Rivage and one we raffled off a mink jacket donated to us from one of my best friends David, and a pair of gold earrings.

At the start of the trial, October 2, 1999, I bought yards of green ribbon and straight pins. Everyone that enter the courtroom in support of Nas with the help of friends we pinned the ribbon on the coat lapel or jacket. They knew the day they could attend the trial they must wear the ribbon to identify the people who sat in the packed courtroom were in support of Nas. The green ribbons had so much impact that the District Attorney said to the investigator—"That mother has too much control." Just imagine a courtroom filled with a sea of supporters all wearing "green ribbons." There were so many people supporting us in many different ways. With gratitude, I recall Cheryl had a friend who had never even met me but sent a check for five hundred dollars.

During the 18 months we were raising funds, there was never an occasion when a single check bounced. That's absolutely amazing.

Here was a clear sign of a friend helping me to see I had to hold my head above the water to survive. Dr. Rosa called one day asking what I was doing, "Sleep," I said. Without saying anything else she showed up at my door un-announced. When I heard the knock at the door I hesitated but knew I had to open the door because it was her. I was in a daze hadn't eaten and showered in days.

"Aginah it's roasting in here," she said. "Aginah, this isn't healthy." She began to open the drapes to allow the sunshine in after turning down the heat.

"Aginah get in the shower." I showered put on sweat pants and sneakers and a jacket. I really didn't want to leave my warm bed and surely not leave the house but I did for Rosa. She drove us to a park near my home. We sat near a stream and watched the fish and listen to the sounds of the water from the stream. She talked and I listened. Just being out of the house and sitting near the stream. It was soothing. That day Rosa had helped me to think that awareness of my depression was the way out. The truth is she gave me something that I didn't have—awareness. I had to take care of myself in order to help my daughter and her three children, my dear grandchildren.

(Actual letter to supporters)

December 1999
Aginah says thank you

Dear Supporters,

The sacred writings reveal to us that, "To everything there is a season," and I have come to my season of Joy, because I know that I am exceedingly blessed.

When I look back over 49 years I see the work of so many people in every step I have taken, and I am amazed. I see the magnitude of family, those born-into-your-life and individuals who stand by you not just because it's a blood thing, but because they chose to be there for you through every milestone.

It means something to be able to say, "That's my sister, my brother, mother, father, cousin, niece, nephew, aunt, uncle, daughter, son, godchild, godmother." I look back, and it feels so good, because it's about Love—unconditional Love.

In the time it takes to blink, I can bring back the "Good Old Days," when the foundation of my life was being built by friendships that began in childhood, at a time when nothing mattered except that everybody clicked in school, on the telephone, at the parties at Omega by the sea and everywhere in Philly girls gathered to make time stand still, for just a while.

And these friendships have endured everything—sometimes held me together-right up to this very day.

I have been blessed by clients and co-workers who made the salon a home-place where I could be myself and look forward to every single appointment and every single day that brought a familiar face through the door. I can count at least two hundred stylists, assistants and receptionists over twenty two years who have stood side-by-side with me, through the good and not-so-good times.

Each has added immeasurably to my life, and I have grown in many ways because they were with me, working it all out.

And Who Are These Sisterfriends, Brotherfriends, and Extended family, Family Members, Clients and Co-workers? They Are You? You are the reason for my season of joy. Without you, the past forty nine would have felt like a half-century instead of a fleeting journey, and I would not have had the strength to face the trials that have been set before me.

As you know the past eighteen months have been the most painful, and stressful time of my entire life. But God has been merciful and brought me out in Victory. I know that my victory would not have been achieved except for you because you responded so willingly to God's plan for my life by surrounding me with Love, loyalty and an awesome outpouring of support as I struggled to win Nas' freedom.

I will never forget the prayers, letters and money raised, or the precious time taken out of your days to be with me in court. I never felt alone in my troubles. I will always remember how you supported me daily, and gave me the strength to battle on, through the tears, the fears, and what seemed like a wall of frustration. I am eternally grateful to you and can never fully repay you. But from the bottom of my heart, I thank you.

I invite everyone to join me in Nassau, Bahamas to start the next chapter of my life by celebrating another Victory, my fiftieth birthday.

This is my millennium moment, because it marks the end of the season and the beginning of the rest of my journey. I want you to sit on the beach with me, soak up the sounds of God's great peace and enjoy the simplicity of sun, sea, and sand. I hope you can join me for this celebration-at-the-beach and to the next one thousand years and another season.

Peace be with you always for the love you've shown me. I will always love you.

Sincerely,
Aginah Carter-Shabazz

Chapter Sixteen

The Trial

Nas Speaks

Roger King, the premier assistant district attorney, really wanted me to testify against Darryl. He even tried to get me to plead guilty in exchange for a lesser sentence. That man is crazy. He called me a small shark and accused me of running with the big sharks. He remembered me from when Rick my children's father was arrested.

Kareem, the private investigator hired by my mother, told her and the fund-raising committee he discovered that the real killers were a couple of guys from Detroit whom Darryl had befriended. They belonged to a gang called "Best Friends," an organization of drug dealers and hit men.

Aginah Speaks

Nas was on trial with two codefendants, Darryl Coleman and John Gordon (one of the men from Detroit), and the other was "star witness," Stacey Culbert. This star witness had made a deal to testify against the others in exchange for an eight-year sentence for the death of Randy. This man had killed at least twenty-three people, including a four-year-old child, and enjoyed killing for money.

Prior to his arrest for the murder of Randy Slade, Stacey and Darryl were drug-dealing associates. The prosecutors knew about the association. They found Stacey serving a life sentence in a federal prison on another charge. They used him to build a case against Darryl, playing one pawn against the other. He was perfect for the scheme they had in mind.

Stacey was a cold-blooded killer desperately looking for a way out, willing to sacrifice any and everything to achieve his objective. Prisons are filled with people like him, people who will never leave prison—unless they happen upon a deal offered by an overzealous prosecutor. Such prosecutors use desperate and dangerous convicted killers, dangling before them the hope of reduced sentences in exchange for their false testimony.

On the streets snitching is frowned upon and produces extreme consequences, even death. Death can be a consequence when an indictment can result in serious time or the disruption of an illegal enterprise. But in prison snitching offers the possibility of an early release. Is it worth the risk? Stacey Culbert, like many, saw an opportunity and took it.

Stacey confessed under oath that he put sixteen bullets into Randy's head. He implicated Darryl. He also claimed that Nas hired him to kill Randy.

The wiretaps presented by Federal Agent Coleman were fraudulent evidence. The voice on the tape did not belong to Nas, and the prosecution knew this. They were actually wiretaps from another case involving another female. Tariq happened to be familiar with that case. He had the original transcripts. He recognized them immediately. Were it not for his having those transcripts and knowing to whom the voice really belonged, Nas could have spent the rest of her life in prison.

I was nervous and anxious. I wanted immediate resolution. I wanted Tariq to show how Roger King railroaded my daughter using fabricated evidence. I wanted Nas home with her children. But Tariq constantly reminded me that he was the lawyer, and I am not. I had to battle with him while waiting for the appropriate time. I had to witness the deceit and manufacturing of lies that went on throughout the trial.

The night before the trial I went to the home of Collette to pick up an outfit she had purchased for Nas. Then I went home. I didn't sleep at all. I was totally restless.

I looked out the window and I saw the thread of light in the sky, letting me know it was time for Morning Prayer. I took a shower, put on my cloak and scarf, and made prayer. I asked God for all the things my grandmother Leslie had told me to pray for just before she died. She told me to ask God to change the heart of the prosecutor and allow the jurors to see the lies and the manipulation taking place in the courtroom.

The last thing she said was "Be strong and get yourself together because Nas is going to be okay. Your grandchildren need you." She lay in the St. Ignatius Nursing Home bed waiting for God to take her home. She kept looking at the ceiling, looking toward heaven. She asked God what He was waiting for. Then she apologized, saying, "When it is my time, You will take me home." A few hours later God took her.

I prayed a prayer for her that God have mercy on her and grant her Paradise. I prayed that my daughter was making prayer at the same time I was making prayer. Although my dad was always in the courtroom in support of my daughter and me, I asked God to give me the strength to bear the courtroom drama without my security blankets—my mother and my grandmother.

I walked to the front of the courtroom and knocked on the door where prisoners were detained before court. I gave the clothes to the guard. Then I sat down in the empty courtroom on the right-hand side after thinking back to when I performed my ablution by washing the right hand first, a practice that reminds us of our duty to uphold what is right.

I kept looking at my watch, anxious for the trial to begin. Tariq finally arrived. He touched my shoulder.

"Are you okay?"

"I'm not good," I told him.

"I'm also a little nervous, but we're going to win this case, God willing."

Then the investigator, Kareem, came into the room.

He said, "Aginah, you look so worried. Everything is going to be all right. We got this."

"I know but . . ."

Court convened at ten o'clock. The jurors slowly filed into the courtroom and took their seats. The bailiff announced the judge and told everyone to rise. The sheriff brought Nas out. He sat her on the right side of the courtroom at the lawyer's table next to Tariq. She turned around to look at the crowded courtroom and saw that the right side of the courtroom was packed with her green ribbon-wearing supporters.

Nas wore a long blue skirt with a light blue shirt. Her hair was pulled up in a bun. I stared at her thinking how much she looked like my mother, especially wearing that hairstyle. She had on black-framed prescription glasses, giving her a professional look. I moved my seat from the first row to the third row center of the courtroom so I could reserve seats for my friends, family, and supporters.

A burly white sheriff brought Stacey Culbert in and sat him in the witness section. Stacy was about six feet tall with an athletic build—an ex-marine. He had dark smooth skin with nice features. His hair was cut neatly. He had a crazed smirk on his face. He looked at his friend, the other co-defendant, John Gordon, and smiled. John nodded back.

The trial twisted and turned, distorting truth and justice. I sat there enduring a menacing charade. The lies, insinuations, and threats were in stereo surround bouncing off the walls and inside my head, making me fearful and sick.

Read the trial transcript and see the unfolding with surprise after surprise.

Chapter Seventeen

Trial Transcripts

Excerpts from the trial transcripts
(These are the original trial transcripts and are written verbatim as typed by the court stenographer.)

(Excerpt)
(Testimony of Stacey Culbert)

October 19, 1999
Courtroom 305, Criminal Justice Center Philadelphia, Pennsylvania

---

Appearances:
Roger King, ESQ.: Premier Assistant District attorney for the commonwealth
William T. Cannon ESQ., and Christopher Warren, ESQ.: For defendant Darryl Coleman
Tariq El-Shabazz, ESQ.: For defendant Yonzetta Hudson
Donald M. Padova, ESQ. Court-appointed counsel for defendant John Gordon

---

Stacey Culbert, called as a witness on behalf of the commonwealth, having been duly sworn, was examined and testified as follows:

Direct examination

By Roger King:
Q: Mr. Culbert, are you currently incarcerated?
A: Yes, Sir, I am
Q: Where are you incarcerated? In a federal facility?
A: Yes, Sir. That's correct

Q: What sentence are you serving?
A: Life
Q: Do you know the defendant in this case, Darryl Coleman?
A: Yes, I do, Sir.
Q: You ever engage in any business with him?
A: Yes, Sir.
Q: What kind of business?
A: Drugs.
Q: Do you know the defendant Yonzetta Hudson?
A: Yes, Sir.
Q: How do you know her?
A: Through Darryl Coleman.
Q: Were you arrested and charged with the killing of William Slade?
A: Yes, Sir
Q: Did you participate in that killing?
A: Yes, Sir, I did.
Q: Did you participate with anyone in this courtroom?
A: Yes, Sir I did.
Q: Who?
A: Darryl Coleman, John Gordon, and Yonzetta Hudson.
Q: What role did Miss Hudson play?
A: She arranged it.
Q: By arranging it, what do you mean?
A: She called Darryl Coleman, A.K.A. Tubs, the day of the incident telling him—

Mr. El-Shabazz: Objection

By Mr. King:
Q: During the course—

The Court: Overruled.
Mr. El-Shabazz: Telephone conversation, your honor.
The court: I don't know whether it's a telephone conversation or not. He said it as though it was a fact. I don't know what he's about to say.

By Mr. King:
Q: After you got off the phone, did you accompany him to a location?
A: Yes, Sir I did.

Q: Somewhere in Germantown. I'm Not exactly sure of the streets. Chelten, or something of that nature. I'm not sure. It was a hair salon, Cleaners.
Q: And when you accompanied him, who went?
A: It was me, Darryl, and John Gordon.
Q: And at that time and at that location did you see Yonzetta Hudson.?
A: Yes. At that time she came out of the building and stood next to the car talking to Tubs.
Q: And what did she say?
A: Well, I didn't hear any of that conversation at that time.
Q: All right. Did you see her again?
A: yes, Sir, I did.
Q: When did you see her?
A: Over her house later that evening.
Q: And what did you talk about?
A: Talked about some money she had that belonged to Randy, and she told Tubs basically what he had said earlier about—

Mr. El-Shabazz: Objection. Move to strike

By Mr. King:
Q: What did they say? What did you hear her say?
A: That she had some money belonged to a gentleman by the name of Randy, and she was looking to get rid of him, and we could have the money if we helped get rid of him.
Q: And what kind of money are we talking about?
A: Fifty grand, a little better. Between fifty and a hundred grand.
Q: And where was this, did you actually see the money?
A: Yes, sir, I did
Q: Tell the ladies and gentlemen of the jury how Randy Slade was killed.
A: When he came to the house and knocked on the door, she didn't let him in. He walked off the porch. At that time I came from on the side of the house. He turned to run, I started firing, and then John and Tubbs followed him. They continued to shoot him.
Q: Did you agree to plead guilty for role in the murder of William also known as Randy Slade?
A: Yes, sir.
Q: And your agreement was for 20 to 40 years?
A: Yes, sir
Q: To run at the same time as your federal life sentence; is that correct?
A: Yes, sir
Q: Nothing further

Cross-examination
By Tariq El-Shabazz
By Mr. Shabazz:

Q: You had been on the run for other murder's is that correct?
A: Yes, Sir
Q: and you were on the run, so you needed money; is that correct?
A: That's correct
Q: And so you're telling the ladies and gentlemen of the jury that because you were broke, you found a way to make some money; is that right?
A: That's correct.
Q: And you went to a location after Mr. Coleman received a page; is that correct?
A: That's correct
Q: Now, the location you went to was where? Tell me about this location Sir. Where was it?
A: It was in some part of Germantown. I don't know the area real well.
Q: Describe the building.
A: It was a house, I guess, single occupancy.
Q: Is that where the beauty salon is?
A: No.
Q: We're going to talk about the house in a minute. Talk about the beauty salon. Where was the salon?
A: Located somewhere around Montgomery drive, Chelten avenue.
Q: But you're familiar with how the building looked?
A: Yes.
Q: Tell me how the building looked, sir?
A: Somewhat of an apartment nature, maybe four or five stories. It has a driveway that comes around with a window in the front.
Q: Four or five stories? It's not bigger than that?
A: I wouldn't be exactly sure on that. I wouldn't want you to hold me accountable.
Q: I'm going to hold you accountable for what you said you saw. You went to that location where there was a meeting; is that correct?
A: Yes.
Q: when you went to that location, you indicated there was a beauty salon?
A: A beauty salon, dry cleaner, something of that nature.
Q: I think you indicated—well, strike that. What type of driveway was it? Was it on the street?
A: No it wasn't
Q: It was shoehorn; is that right?
A: Yes. Something like that.

Q: And that's where you went? The day that this murder was committed, that's where you went?
A: yes.
Q: And you are as sure about that as you are about that as you are about the rest of your testimony; is that right?
A: From the information that I was given, yes, I am.
Q: hold it. Hold, hold, hold. You were there, weren't you?
A: Yeah.
Q: So you don't tell me about information you were given.
A: I didn't go inside. I stayed out at the car, so I wouldn't know . . .
Q: Well, you didn't say that when you talked to Mr. King, did you?
A: I told him what I thought it was.
Q: and you said that at this spot there was a salon; is that right?
A: Yes. A salon or cleaners, something of that.
Q: I'm sorry. A salon or cleaners. And the person came out of that building; is that right?
A: Yes.
Q: And this is a high-rise building; is that right?
A: Yes. Four or five stories.
Q: And, in fact, there was an oval-shaped driveway that you drive in; is that right?
A: yes.
Q: Now you are sure about that, is that right?
A: Yes
Q: And that's where you went; is that correct?
A: That is were I went.
Q: And you are as sure about that as you are the rest of your testimony, not based on something someone told you?
A: Not something.
Q: In fact, I think you gave a little more detail. Wasn't the location—did the location of this area, of this building or this salon or apartment building, or whatever you were told or what you saw, was it at a dead end or was there, another street or was it a two-way street or a one-way street? Tell us, Sir, what was it?
A: if I recall correctly, it was a two-way or may have been a one-way. It was a store down at the end of it, because when we left there, we went down, like, in and out, something of that nature, where it was a dry cleaner, or something.

Mr. Shabazz asks for a photo of the building to be marked d-3 for identification. The photograph is then showed to Stacy Culbert.

Q: Do you recognize that?
A: Yes, I do. It doesn't look like the building I remember.
Q: So how do you remember the building?
A: At the time I don't think this awning was on it.
Q: But that's the building you went to without the awning; is that right?
A: Possibly.
Q: Don't give me possibly. Do you remember?
A: The windows yes. I would concede that this is it.
Q: thank you sir, and that's the building you went to where the salon was—excuse me, Sir, where the salon was where you indicate my client met with Mr. Coleman; is that right?
A: Yes
Q: Okay. Let's talk about the house you went to. Can you describe the house you went to?
A: It was a single dwelling. All the houses in Philly are connected together. I mean, when you say describe—
Q: I wasn't there. You told the ladies and gentlemen you were there, you went to the house. Describe it. When you opened the front door, Sir, did you remember seeing any of the furniture?
A: Yes
Q: what color furniture did you see?
A: To be honest, I can't remember that.
Q: you don't recall the color of the furniture that you see in the house. Okay. Was there any furniture or boxes?
A: It was furniture in the house.
Q: Well, where were her daughters?
A: I don't know.
Q: Well, was her son there?
A: I didn't see anyone in the house but her.
Q: And the floor, was it hardwood, carpeted, or linoleum?
A: I think it was carpeted.
Q: What color was the carpet? You were in this house? What color was the carpet?
A: I can't recall
Q: I'm sure you can. You remember everything else. Did she have stairs or escalator?
A: Stairs
Q: where were the stairs located in the house?
A: back to the right hand side, I think.

Q: Oh. So right from where—right from—is it on the right hand side from the front door? Is it the right-hand side from the back door? Is it the right-and side from the kitchen? Where is it on the—
A: From the front door, stairs would be located on the right-hand side.
Q: Were those carpeted or hardwood?
A: If I remember correctly, it was carpeted.
Q: Do you remember the color paint?
A: I think the house was white, painted.
Q: Do you think or do you know?
A: Well, I really don't go into a house and do a color inspection, or anything, Mr. Shabazz.
Q: Well, I'm sure you didn't do a color inspection. You can't tell me the color of the carpet or the bed that the individual was laying on when you shot him in the head could you?
A: No I couldn't.
Q: And you can't tell me what color clothing the three-year old girl had on when she got shot in the head; is that right.
A: No, I couldn't
Q: Do you recall whether or not the house was lit by an overhead light or were there lamps?
A: No, I do not.
Q: How long did you stay in the house?
A: Maybe ten, fifteen minutes.
Q: Okay. And during that ten or fifteen minute period of time you indicated that my client brought up a bag of money; is that right?
A: Yes, she did.
Q: Okay. And she showed you this bag of money; is that right?
A: Yes, sir
Q: And how much money was in the bag?
A: Approximately, I'll say, fifty grand or maybe a little more.
Q: Wasn't a hundred grand?
A: no.
Q: Wasn't two hundred grand?
A: No. I didn't count the money.
Q: So where did you get this approximation of fifty grand if you didn't count the money?
A: Well, I did a quick visual. She poured it out on the table.
Q: And how was it when she poured it out?
A: It was bundled.
Q: Bundled? How many bundles?
A: Maybe seven or eight.

Q: And the guns, where did you go to get these guns?
A: I think down by Baltimore Pike, or something. It was in West Philly, over a house where Vernon was.
Q: And—I'm sorry. You said Vernon was?
A: Yes.
Q: So Vernon Daniels was at the house when the guns were retrieved?
A: Where we retrieved the guns from, Vernon Daniels was at that house. Yes.
Q: Now, you indicated that you believe it was $50,000; is that right? Somewhere around there; is that correct?
A: Yes. I think I said between fifty and a hundred thousand in my statement.
Q: Oh, Oh. You know where I was going, huh? Well, you indicated that at certain times that she poured it on the table; is that correct?
A: That is correct.
Q: Okay. And you testified under oath at a preliminary hearing, did you not?
A: I did.
Q: And at that preliminary hearing you were asked questions by Mr. King who was there at this time; is that correct?
A: Yes, sir.
Q: And an attorney for Miss Hudson who was there at that time; is that right?
A: Yes, sir
Q: And that was back on May 20th, 1998; is that correct?
A: Yes, sir.
Q: Do you recall ever telling anyone that she poured it out on the table?
A: I don't know if I mentioned it?
Q: You don't know if you mentioned it?
A: No.
Q: Do you remember whether or not you told anyone in any statement, and Mr. King showed you about three statements, that Miss Hudson poured money out on the table?
A: I don't know if I said it.
Q: Well, Sir, let me help you out. You never said it.
A: Okay.
Q: And this table, was it a coffee table, an end table, or kitchen table?
A: Dining room table.
Q: Dining room table?
A: Yes.
Q: And of course, you don't recall how that looks, either?
A: Actually, I do
Q: Oh. How did that look?
A: It was a white linoleum type table, gold trimming.

Q: And you are sure about that as you are about the rest of your testimony; is that right? What kind of bag was it that you indicated this money was in?
A: Somewhat like the bag that's sitting over here by the stenographer, a bag like that.
Q: For the record, you would agree with me this is a plastic bag?
A: Yes.
Q: Sort of like a shopping bag; is that right?
A: yes
Q: And you weren't able to see through the bag, where you?
A: See through the bag. No. No, I didn't see through the bag.
Q: Now, you indicated you came in contact with $50,000 because you know denominations of money; is that correct?
A: Yes.
Q: And you know how money is wrapped; is that right?
A: Yes. That is correct
Q: Never counted the money?
A: No.
Q: No one ever told you it was that amount; is that right?
A: No. She mentioned an amount, but I—
Q: Oh. She mentioned an amount?
A: Yes.
Q: what amount did she mention?
A: I can't recall, so I'm not going to speculate.
Q: Okay. Did you ever tell—strike that. Now, you indicated at some point you took a certain position outside the home; is that right?
A: Yes.
Q: And that was across the street; is that correct?
A: That was on the same side that her house was located but maybe three or four houses down.
Q: Now, did you have a car, by the way?
A: Yes, we did.
Q: Okay. What kind of car did you have?
A: I had a Taurus rental.
Q: who rented the car?
A: A female friend of mine.
Q: Female friend? Your wife?
A: Female friend
Q: Okay. Your wife lives in Philly, too; is that right?
A: Yes.

Q: Okay. And she would rent cars for you, too is that right?
A: Yes.
Q: And it's your testimony that you and three other people went to my client's house; is that right?
A: That is correct.
Q: And you rang the doorbell; is that right?
A: That is correct.
Q: And she came in—or ya'll came in; is that correct?
A: That is correct.
Q: Where was the doorbell? On the right-hand side or left-hand side?
A: I didn't ring the doorbell. I think Tubbs rang the doorbell. It was his friend.
Q: So he rung the doorbell though?
A: To my recollection, I think he did. Yes.
Q: And you are as sure about that as you are about the rest of your testimony? Approximately what time did you go to this location?
A: To her home?
Q: Yes, sir
A: I'll say maybe ten or eleven.
Q: Did you ever go to see a car that was parked?
A: Yes, we did.
Q: Well, I'm not asking about we. I'm talking about you.
A: Yes, I did.
Q: Okay. And what time did you do that?
A: I think it was maybe eleven or twelve then.
Q: what time was it; can you tell the ladies and gentlemen, that you went to this location where the salon was?
A: Between six and seven in the evening.
Q: What day of the week was this?
A: Saturday.
Q: Sure a bout that?
A: Yes
Q: Now, do you remember me asking you maybe about six questions ago about the denominations of the money? Remember that?
A: Yes, I do.
Q: And you indicated that Miss Hudson said the denominations of the money, but you don't recall?
A: Yes

The tipstaff: Page 63, counsel, preliminary hearing.

Q: Do you remember this question? "At any time while you were in there," speaking of the house, 'Did anyone say how much money was in the bag?" You answered, "No, it wasn't said how much money it was." Do you remember that question and giving that answer?
A: Yes, I do.
Q: And when you were asked that question and you gave that answer, you were under oath; is that right?
A: Yes,
Q: You put your hand on that book; is that correct?
A: That's correct.
Q: And you swore to tell the truth; is that correct?
A: That's what I'm doing.
Q: well, you just told us eight questions ago that Miss Hudson said an amount.
A: Yes, I did.
Q: You remember that? But you said back at the preliminary hearing that no one said how much it was. You remember that?
A: I can't recall.
Q: You want to see it?
A: If it would help.
Q: Sure. On the day that you testified at the preliminary hearing, you were Stacey Culbert that day?
A: Yes, sir
Q: You didn't use an alias?
A: No, Sir, I didn't
Q: Does the question read exactly how I read it?
A: Yes, it does.
Q: Does the answer read exactly how I read it?
A: Yes, it does.
Q: Were you under oath that day?
A: Yes, sir I was
Q: Is that the answer you gave?
A: Yes
Q: Which truth are you telling? The truth you're telling today or the truth you told us back then?
Mr. King: Objection!
The court: Sustained!

Aginah

The following testimony features Randy Slade's mother and brother. Prosecutor Roger King attempts to create both motives for Randy's murder as well as attempting to place Nas's involvement in his murder from the mother, Clara Slade's testimony.

I was expecting to see Mr. and Mrs. Slade. Tariq had already briefed me that they would be testifying today. I was in the hallway when they arrived. Mrs. Slade walks in and Mr. Slade stops in front of me.

"I know your husband Brother Gerald, I know him very well," he said.

"You mean my ex-husband, so why are you going to tell lies against my daughter?" I asked.

He said, "I'm not testifying against your daughter, my wife is."

When I saw his wife leaving out of the courtroom, I walked out behind her and followed her to the bathroom. I waited for her to come out of the stall.

"Good morning, Mrs. Slade, I am Yonzetta's mother."

She just stood there as if I had some nerve.

"I'm sorry for what happened to your son, but my daughter had nothing to do with his murder and as a mother to another I can imagine your pain having someone taking your son's life, so imagine mine. You're taking my daughter away from me and her children."

She just rolled her eyes and made her way back into the courtroom.

Testimony of Clara Slade and Michael Slade
October 20, 1999
Courtroom 305, Criminal Justice Center
Philadelphia, Pennsylvania
Before: The honorable James A. Lineberger, J. and Jury
Appearances:

Roger King, ESQ. Premier Assistant district attorney for the commonwealth
William T. Cannon, ESQ For defendant Darryl Coleman
Tariq El-Shabazz, ESQ for defendant Yonzetta Hudson

Cross-examination by Mr. Cannon

Q: Mrs. Slade, you've never testified before in the matter; am I correct about that?

A: That's correct.

Q: This is the first time; is that right?

A: Yes.

Q: And your testifying about a telephone conversation that you say happened on April 2nd of 1994; is that correct?

A: April 1st on Good Friday.

Q: April 1st. Did you say Good Friday?

A: Yes

Q: Now, here we are in October of 1999, about 5-1/2 years later, and you're trying to remember what happened 5-1/2 years ago; am I right?
A: I don't have to try. It's stamped I my head
Q: Stamped in your head?
A: Yes.
Q: All right. And so what you clearly remember 5-1/2 years later, you certainly would remember two weeks later, am I right, that is, two weeks after your son was killed, you'd certainly remember it then, wouldn't you?
A: (no response)
Q: Is that a yes or a no?
A: I would remember two weeks later, two weeks what?
Q: About the contents of this conversation?
A: Yes
Q: Okay. Now, on the day that Randy was killed, you did not speak with the police on that day in any formal setting; is that right?
A: The day he was killed, Officer Engenlauf came to my house
Q: Okay, did he take a statement from you?
A: No he just brought the message.
Q: Okay, however, on April 15th, almost two weeks later, detective Egenlauf returned to your home at 7100 Limekiln Pike and interviewed you; is that correct?
A: Yes.
Q: At this time he wrote down what you had to say; is that right?
A: Yes.
Q: Now, have you seen a copy of your interview as taken on April the 15th of 1995?
A: No, I haven't.
Q: Mr. King never showed it to you?
A: I didn't see it.
Q: You've never seen it, I suppose?
A: Wait a minute. The statement that—
Q: Permit me to do this Mrs. Slade—
A: Okay
Q: To assist you
A: Okay
Q: Mrs. Slade, take a look at that and see if you can tell us what that document is?
A: Oh, yeah, I saw this, but it had April 2nd on it, and that's why I thought there was another report, or something, with April 14th

Q: Well this particular report you've just been shown is dated April 2nd, 1994; is that right?
A: Well, on this paper it says April 2nd, and that's what was on my paper.
Q: Can you show me where you're indicating?

The Court: no, see that's the death of William Slade is April 2nd.
Mrs. Slade: Oh yeah, there's the date I'm sorry.

Q: What is the date?
A: April 15th
Q: 1994?
A: Yes. That is the statement that I saw. I just overlooked the date.
Q: Well, this is the statement that you gave on April 15th, 1994; is that correct?
A: Yes.
Q: Now, you're saying you saw this before. Where did you see it?
A: I saw it—I saw it in the room out there.
Q: The room out there? You mean the room outside the courtroom?
A: Yes.
Q: Was that today?
A: No.
Q: Was it yesterday?
A: It was a couple of days ago.
Q: All right. A couple days ago. And did detective Egenlauf give you a copy of that?
A: No.
Q: Did some detective give you a copy of that?
A: Somebody handed it to me.
Q: Did you read it at that time?
A: I just looked at it because I know the truth and I can say the truth a thousand times and I didn't have to read it.
Q: I see, so you glanced at it?
A: Yes
Q: Didn't read it?
A: No.
Q: Why was it given to you, if you know?
A: I don't know. I don't have to read it.
Q: where you told that this was going to be given to you?
A: They just said, "This is your statement that you gave."

Q: They wanted you to read it, didn't they?
A: yes, they wanted me to read it
Q: And you wouldn't read it?
A: No I didn't read it all.
Q: Why not?
A: Because I know the truth, and when I get up here, I can tell you the truth over and over.
Q: You mean, Mrs. Slade, before you even read this document; you knew not to read it because you knew this document would make you look like a liar?
A: I'm not—
Q: Is that why you refused to read the statement?
A: I'm not a liar.
Q: I didn't call you one
A: Look like a liar
Q: would you turn to page 2 and you see the question at the top, it says, "Did Randy tell you where he was going the night he was killed?" Do you see that question?
A: Yes
Q: I want you to read the answer that is recorded on this statement. The one that detective Egenlauf recorded in your home on April 15th, 1994—
A: Yes
Q: Which reads, "My husband overheard a conversation Randy has with Darryl on the phone right before he left the house and Randy told Darryl he would meet with her later." Did I read that correctly?
A: Yes
Q: Now did you tell that to detective Engenlauf back on April 15th, 1994?
A: yes I did
Q: You didn't tell detective Egenlauf, I heard a conversation that randy had? Did you?
A: I didn't tell him that, no.
Q: Why would you say that your husband heard a conversation instead of reporting to the detective that you heard it?
A: Because my husband heard the whole conversation and he had more to tell him than I did, and I only heard bits and pieces with Darryl's name and answering with Naz's name. So my husband was in the room the whole time, so I thought it would be better, in case one of us had to get on the stand, for my husband to tell the whole content of the conversation instead of me in little pieces.

Q: You didn't think it was appropriate to mention to the detective that you heard a part of the conversation, is that your testimony?
A: Well, during that time I was, like really sick, and I just told him what I—what my husband had heard.
Q: Instead of what you say you heard; is that right?
A: Yes. Well, we both heard parts of it.
Q: Now your husband is he still alive, I hope?
A: Yes
Q: Is he here today?
A: Yes
Q: what tine of the day or evening was this call received, Mrs. Slade?
A: Around—between, I guess 7 and 7:30. Around 7:30.
Q: Now you're the mother of Randy Slade and you would like to see all three of these people convicted for the death of your son; is that correct?
A: I would like to see justice done. I would like to see—yes I would like to see justice done.
Q: Justice done in your mind is for everybody to be convicted; is that right?
A: Well, if you do something wrong, I think you should be punished for it, so yes.
Q: So you decided to help the case by testifying to something that your husband heard but you did not; is that correct?
A: I heard it

Mr. Cannon: Nothing further.
The Court: Mr. Shabazz?
Mr. Shabazz: Just one, your honor if I might
By Mr. Shabazz:
Q: The same page 2 of that document you have before you, you were asked a question by detective Egenlauf, and the question was, the last question, "Has Yonzetta Hudson ever called your home?" Do you see that question down there, Ma'm?
A: Yes
Q: Your answer was, "All the time she would call;" Is that correct?
A: Yes
Q: Nowhere in that statement did you indicate, oh, by the way, she called the night that my son was killed. Did you say that in the statement at all, Ma'am?
A: No

Q: Nowhere in this statement have you ever indicated that Yonzetta Hudson called and you answered the phone and you gave the phone to your son that night. Is it in the statement, Ma'am?
A: I told him, like, back from the front page.
Q: That Yonzetta Hudson called?
A: Yes
Q: On the front page?
A: I answered the phone.
Q: Ma'am, I'd just like you to listen to my question. In that document that you have before you, on that front page or the second page, did you ever tell detective Egenlauf that Yonzetta Hudson called your house that night?
A: No, I didn't tell him, but I answered the phone

Mr. Shabazz: Thank you, ma'am I have nothing further.

Michael Slade, called as a witness on behalf of the commonwealth, having been duly sworn, was examined and testified as follows:

Direct examination

By Mr. King:
Q: Mr. Slade, I'd like to direct your attention initially to December the 20th of 1993. Did something happen on that day that brings you to court today?
A: Yes it did
Q: Could you relate, for the benefit of the ladies and gentlemen of the jury, what happened?
A: it was approximately, I would say, Mid-morning, my mother and father and I were speaking, going back and forth just general conversation. We had just awakened and we were all in the living room area seated speaking with one another, basically, going over a review of what we were going to do on that day. At that particular time my brother Randy came into the house, and we spoke with him just briefly, and he said that he had to leave out, and he as headed to his girlfriend's beauty salon. And then approximately not even a half minute, we heard gunshots had erupted at that time, and at that time we heard two to three gunshots.
Q: what did you do after hearing two to three gunshots?
A: I ran directly to the bay window.
Q: A when you ran directly to the bay window what, if anything did you see?
A: I seen a car, and basically, guys were shooting at Randy at that particular point in time. Then the one gentleman jumped out the car, and he

proceeded to continue to shoot at Randy. And we both looked—I looked at both sides. Of course, I was—I was hoping my brother would be okay.

Q: Do you see anyone in court here today who you saw at that time?

A: Yes, I do. It's right here. The defendant right here, Coleman (indicating).

Exhibit shown to the jury

By Mr. King:

Q: Mr. Slade, could you take a moment and look at that exhibit? Do you recognize the vehicle shown there?

A: Yes I do.

Q: And what Vehicle is that?

A: It's my brother's. It's the car that my brother had at the time of the incident.

Q: And what was it. What make and what year?

A: Lexus 400 SE, 1992

Q: On these photographs, can you see any damage to this Lexus Automobile?

A: Yes, I see piercing bullet holes all throughout, interior and exterior of the car.

Cross Examination

By Mr. King:

Q: Mr. Slade, I have a little difficulty following your testimony about your brother coming into some money, coming into a hundred or two hundred thousand dollars.

A: I can only speculate on that

Q: Where that hundred thousand dollars came from. Are you able to say, Mr. Slade, my brother was a drug dealer? Are you able to say that because I never witnessed him make a transaction, so I could only say, I could never know what he actually did.

A: I could still only be speculating. I wasn't sure.

Q: Well, how do you know he came into a hundred or two hundred thousand dollars? How do you know?

Cross-examination

By Mr. Cannon:

Q: Your brother's Lexus was shot up on March the 29th of 1994, just three days before he was killed; isn't that so sir?

A: Yes.

Q: And the bullet holes in those photographs represent the bullets of those shots being fired on March 29th, 1994, don't they?
A: Yes.
Q: And Darryl Coleman and nobody at this table had anything to do with shooting up this Lexus on March 29, 1994, did they?
A: Yes, on March—March, that's the date in question?
Q: March 29, 1994.
A: No. Not to my knowledge I do not know that. Right
Q: Okay. Now, how did you learn your brother had been killed?
A: My mother
Q: Mr. Slade, sometime that day you went to the police station; is that right?
A: Yes sir.
Q: That is the date you learned of your brother's death?
A: Yes
Q: And you learned that my client Darryl Coleman had been arrested by the detective that day; is that right?
A: It was told to us they had someone in custody.
Q: Someone in custody?
A: Yes.
Q: Well, didn't they give you a name?
A: Not at that point in time no.
Q: I mean, that was the occasion when you told them about something happening back in December of '93; right?
A: Right
Q: And that was the first time you told the police officer anything with that name Darryl Coleman; right?
A: Well, I spoke with the officers and told them there was an incident outside my parents' house at that point in time.
Q: You told them about that on April 2nd, 1994, the day you went down to homicide; right?
A: yes.
Q: And that was only after they informed you that Darryl Coleman had been arrested; isn't that right?
A: They didn't say any names to me at all
Q: Tell me about the relationship between your brother and Darryl Coleman.
A: Well, when I first learned about the situation, that Randy and Darryl had encountered each other, it was through the girl that Randy was seeing at that particular time. And I only got bits and pieces and parts of what he was trying to tell me at that time. Basically, it was he had met, he thought, at that time a decent female that he could trust.

Q: Mr. Slade, I have your statement that you gave to police on April 2nd, 1994. And have you seen that, had a chance to read that?
A: Yes. Yeah I seen it. I previously browsed it.
Q: And so after you had described the guy that you saw shooting at your brother, you remember the detective asked you if you know this guy from anywhere, and you said, no, you had never seen him, remember giving that answer?
A: Yes.
Q: So you were telling him, the detective, the man shooting at your brother on December 20, '93, was somebody you'd never seen before; is that true?
A: Before that time? Excuse me. You said before that time?
Q: Of course. Somebody you had never seen before December 20, 1993?
A: Is that true that I had never seen him before? Is that what you're asking me? I don't understand the question.
Q: Sure. The detective asked you about the man who you had just got done telling them you saw shooting at your brother. The detective said, "Do you know this guy from anywhere?" "Answer. No I had never seen him before" Remember giving your answer?
A: Yes
Q: Was that truthful?
A: Yes
Q: You were called to testify back on May 26th, 1994; is that right
A: Yes
Q: You remember testifying at the hearing?
A: Vaguely
Q: The answer at the bottom of the page that says, "I was looking at who was shooting at him

"Question. At the time that you see this car it was directly in from of you, you don't see Mr. Coleman at that time do you?
"Answer. No I don't.
"Question. Because you had never seen Mr. Coleman before this, had you?"

A: Yes I had seen him before."
Q: Remember giving that answer?
A: That was on what date?

Q: It was in May of 1994; just one month after your brother was killed when you testified under oath that you had seen the man shooting your brother. Well, if that answer was truthful, then why did you tell the detective in your statement that you'd never seen the man before?

A: during that time, that was the morning proceeding, right after my brother—I don't think I was thinking clearly. But some of the answers I might have said may have been adrenaline and because I did—I had seen him before.

Q: Did you also tell the police when you were interviewed on July 28, 1995 that your brother and Darryl Coleman were shooting at each other for a while? Did you tell them that?

A: Yes, I did.

Mr. Cannon: I have nothing further

The court: Weren't there three incidents? My Question is when were these bullet holes put in your brother's car?

The witness: The one before his murder.

The court: which would have been that March incident?

The witness: Yes

The court: So when you looked out your mother's window at your brother being shot at, the damage in these pictures, the damage was not inflicted on that day; right?

The witness: Exactly

The court: the damage reflected in these photographs were from an incident sometime in March?

The witness: Yes, sir

The court: thank you very much. You may step down.

The following wiretaps reveal absolutely nothing, instead are irrelevant in the case and will reveal just how hard Roger King attempted to involve Nas in the orchestrating of Randy Slade.

Once again, I was standing in the hallway when FBI agent Jesse Coleman came up on the elevator. I walked over to him and introduced myself.

"I'm Yonzetta's mother; I'm the one who used to answer the phone when you called for her."

He was a federal agent who was also in the back pocket of the prosecutor. I was told he wined and dined young women to get information about their boyfriends or husbands.

He said, "Oh, how are you, Aginah." Then he walked in the courtroom. Stephanie was with me.

"That's Jesse Coleman, he's supposed to be testifying that he has Nas on wiretap," I said.

Wire taps, FBI agent and Jessie Coleman
(Testimony of special agent Jesse Coleman)
October 21, 1999
Courtroom 305, Criminal Justice Center
Philadelphia, Pennsylvania
Appearances:
Roger King, ESQ.: Premier Assistant District attorney for the commonwealth
William T Cannon ESQ. and Christopher Warren, ESQ.: For defendant Darryl Coleman
Tariq El-Shabazz, ESQ.: For defendant Yonzetta Hudson

Partial Wiretap from Darryl Coleman and Terrence Gibbs and an unknown female:

Darryl Coleman: Get me what I need man you know what I'm saying. That's all I need from you right now nothing else. Lucretia told me somebody shot her wheel up and shit right after that you and boo supposed to call her and see her.

Terrence Gibbs: Uh-huh

Darryl Coleman: Then I hollered back, I was like, damn you didn't tell me you was with the boy Jody and other dudes you were fucking. Anyway just do what I asked, he overlooked the mutherfucking jawn, which states, bang, such and such would have swore he was shot before. He never said who shot him and he never said that he saw him before, whatever, he said the people whipped his best friend before and he killed his nephew and he went and killed whoever killed his nephew. Why would I mutherfucking want to kill him? Because this ain't no robbery or nothing this is based on aspect of anger. Many times he's been shot by multiple mutherfucking guns and shit. Mutherfuckers hated dude foreal. If I had reason to hate him or whatever, who else would want to hate him. In plain fact, he states that he stated to her he tried to kill somebody. He did kill somebody, because somebody killed his nephew. Then in fact, somebody like Keith or whoever, which can be you know take the fall guy position, but they can't charge you know. I hate him like that because he shot me, or tried to kill me, you know what I'm saying. So, you need to get up on that shit. I need to find out from that bitch, because she don't know if they coming or going.

Mr. Shabazz: Judge, my problem is several. One, there's the mention of jawns all trough this. Now, people who have a colloquial background know jawns can be a fax machine, at one time that was a jawn, and throughout the tape we don't know what jawn means. So, judge, what the problem is, Mr Coleman, agent Coleman cant interpret what jawn means at a particular time is either Mr. Coleman himself, and I'm not talking about Jesse Coleman, and/or Mr. Gibbs.

The Court: I understand

Mr. Shabazz: Secondly, your honor, there is numerous mention of bitch.

The court: right.

Mr. Shabazz: And there are names, Lucretia, Kia, Tangy, Michelle, I mean the problem is this judge. I don't want anyone on the jury to assume that when bitch is being said, because bitch has been used and has been used by people to describe, although I don't do that, to describe women. I don't want anyone to actually assume that because my client is sitting here, that Mr. Coleman is having a discussion about my client, Yonzetta Hudson. There has been evidence already put forward that my client was not dealing with Mr. Coleman, that Mr. Coleman had this girlfriend and, in fact, he is talking about marriage.

The court: No I'm not going to permit that. I'm going to permit that, number one, I would think that if the reference to bitch is in there and that she brought me a couple of dollars down here or they promised to bring a couple of dollars, there been testimony that this lady had hundreds of thousands of dollars, so he cant be talking about her. "Her," only brought him a small amount of money.

Mr. Shabazz: Judge, she never had hundreds of thousands of dollars. That's never been established.

Mr. King: your honor, the commonwealth would call as its next witness, special agent Jesse Coleman of the F.B.I.

The next transcript highlights the mutual benefits that sometime exist between law enforcement and prosecutors that often lead to withholding evidence, fabricating facts as well as the actual manufacturing of evidence in the effort to convict at all cost.

Special agent Jesse Coleman, Federal Bureau of Investigation, Philadelphia Division, called as a witness on behalf of the commonwealth, having been duly sworn, was examined and testified as follows:

Direct examination

By Mr. King:

Q: Agent Coleman, I show you what has earlier been marked for identification as commonwealth exhibit 84, 85, 86. Agent Coleman, these three documents that appear in front of you are they authorized wiretaps in the matter of the United States of America Versus Vernon Daniels, Et al?

A: Yes, Sir. That is correct.

Q: Were you the agent in that particular matter?
A: Yes sir, that's correct
Q: and these particular orders covered what phone numbers, sir?
A: Number 84 covered telephone numbers, gave us authorization to wiretap telephone numbers 215-473-1467, which is a telephone subscribed to by Vaughn Davis, also gave us authorization to wiretap telephone number 215-763-9301, which is subscribed by Kim Long, also gave us authorization to wiretap a cellular phone 215-815-8017, which is subscribed to a name Barbara Gibbs.
Q: During the course of the existence of the order from the judge Rendell, were certain communications intercepted involving Terrance Gibbs and Darryl Coleman?
A: Yes, sir. That's correct.
Q: Could you briefly explain for the benefit of the ladies and gentleman of the jury the mechanics of these taps?
A: Yes, sir. The way the equipment is set up, actually getting authorization from a federal judge to tap a phone, the wiretap is installed. Once the person whose phone is tapped picks up the phone, recording begins, the recording begins, a monitor listens to the conversation as its being recorded. When the phone number is dialed, the number dialed appears on the computer screen. It prints out on a printout sheet. When the conversation ends and the phone is put back, the recording automatically stops.
Q: As the assigned case agent, did you become familiar with certain voices that were recorded in as much as you would be able to recognize those voices once the tapes were transcribed?
A: Yes
Q: And did you so note that one the transcripts?
A: Yes, Sir.
Q: Agent Coleman, were certain phone messages intercepted that you appeared here today ready to play for the benefit of the ladies and gentlemen of the jury?
A: Yes, sir that is correct
Q: The first tape is what date agent?
A: December 2nd, 1994, at 11:59 A.M., conversation between Darryl Coleman, Terrance Gibbs, and an unknown female.
Q: Did you bring that tape with you?
A: Yes, sir, I did.
Q: And, your honor, for benefit of the ladies and gentlemen of the jury, the commonwealth will use a computer to enhance this transcript rather than giving them individual copies, and I believe its times so that as the tape is playing officer Trentwith, who's sitting at the keyboard will be referring to the item as depicted.

(Whereupon, Audio tape dated December 2nd, 1994, at 11:59 A.M. played as transcript simultaneously shown on screen)

By Mr. King:
Q: Agent Coleman, whose voice is that, sir.
A: That's Darryl Coleman talking now and the female you here in the background is Kia Long.
Q: And the Vern that's referred to?
A: Vernon Daniels
Q: Who's that speaking?
A: Right now it's Darryl Coleman.
Q: What is happening now Agent?
A: Darryl Coleman made the three-way call from the phone he was on to an unknown female. Now you have Darryl Coleman, Terrence Gibbs, and an unknown female on the line.
Mr. Shabazz: Excuse me, what'd you say? An unknown female on the line?
The witness: Yes

Closing argument of Tariq El-Shabazz, ESQ.
October 27, 1999 Courtroom 305, Criminal Justice Center Philadelphia, Pennsylvania

---

Mr. Shabazz: Your honor, Miss Hudson, members and friends of the Hudson family, counsel to my left, Mr. and Mrs. Slade, Mr. King, Ladies and gentlemen of the jury, good afternoon.
The Jury: Good afternoon
Mr. Shabazz: One of the most difficult things to do is to come up and speak to you after you've heard two other individuals argue to you, especially if the other two individuals are individuals that are involved in a similar case or the same case and they are defense attorneys and you yourself are a defense attorney. It's a difficult thing to do, but as his honor told you from the outset that I represent Yonzetta Hudson. This is who I represent. I don't represent anyone else at this table and with all due respect to the men sitting at this table, my concern is this young lady's life and no one else as it relates to the people in the courtroom. And I say that respectfully, no disrespect of counsel, no disrespect to their clients, but I represent Yonzetta Hudson. That being said, Mr. King said to you in his opening statement, he said, "Ladies and gentlemen, this case will take you from the heights of heaven to the bowels below."

And there was nothing that ever came from this man's mouth that was more poignant, more apropos, more to the point than those words because Mr. King has certainly taken, I don't know if it was the heights of heaven but I can sure you it was bowels of hell. When he brought in Stacy Culbert and told every one of you that this man is a reliable, believable witness in a case that's affecting this young lady's life, that's the bowels of hell.

And ladies and gentlemen, never make a deal wit the devil. Because if you make a deal with the devil, I submit to you, you lose your soul. Why do I say that? Well, when Mr. Culbert took the stand on direct examination, and, you know the funny thing about Mr. Culbert is that Mr. Culbert called me Mr. Shabazz. I never met that man a day in my life. But when I approached him he called me Mr. Shabazz, and it says to me that someone was talking to him about me. Someone was trying to warn him about the truth that I was going to seek. Someone was trying to get into this man's mind to prepare him for the questions that I had for him. But ladies and gentlemen, no matter what they said to him for two weeks, two months, or two years, nothing can prepare you from the truth you saw it with your own eyes and you heard it with your own ears. And what did you hear? On direct examination Mr. king asked him, did you kill such and such? One murder. He says, did you kill such and such, second murder. And he said, yeah, I killed him. And was that self-defense? Do you remember that? Ladies and gentlemen, your recollection controls. And it wasn't until cross examination, and thank God for cross-examination, that you found out that the man that he killed in self-defense was sleeping in his bed when the bullet went into his head. On direct examination he was asked the question about what deals did the commonwealth give you? All they said was such and such. But it wasn't until Cross-examination that you know the commonwealth said more than, "such and such." They said, "we will talk, this is not part of the agreement, but we'll talk to the feds about you." Never make a deal with the devil because if you make a deal with the devil you just may lose your soul.

The man forgot the amount of people he killed, do you remember the question? Cross-examination. Cross-examination. Mr. Culbert, you forgot how many people you killed it was so many. And you remember what his word to me was? Yes. Yes. This man got a deal from the commonwealth for third degree, 20 to 40 years to run simultaneous to any sentence he's serving now, not to face the death penalty, and they want you to put this lady's life on the line because he said something?

Mr. King: Objection
The court: Overruled
Mr. Shabazz: Because he said something?

Ladies and gentlemen, I wasn't here to try to entertain you, and that's not what I was trying to do when I was questioning that man. But that man came in here and looked at me. And when he looked at me he said the house, the house looks this way, the steps on the right side, the walls are white, and the walls had texture on it like popcorn ceilings. Did you remember him saying that to you? He didn't have to say that. He could have said I don't recall. But he was trying to be descriptive to bolster his lie. I was able to put a witness that had nothing to gain, nothing to gain, no record, no alias, nothing to gain.

And what did she tell you? OH no! and you can ask to see these pictures, ladies and gentlemen. There's no textures on that wall, the wall looked with pinkish color on it, the way it looked back in 1994. No, there is no doorbell to ring. There is no back room, ladies and gentlemen. But what there is—is a straight-through house. There is no back room.

But it doesn't stop there. He decided to give details to bolster his lying, tell us a lie. And in telling us a lie he told you. I went to this place that had a circular type parking area, and it was a building, an apartment building. And then I held to him DH-2, and I said look at that. Yes.

Everything except the awning, that's the place that I went to, and I was able to see directly in the salon and I was able to see Yonzetta Hudson come out of the salon and have conversation with Darryl Coleman. That's what he said. But you and I know that there was no salon there in 1994 that the salon came after, years after this incident. You and I know that now.

So how did he get that information? I submit to you someone said it to him. Why? Because this young lady owns the salon there and she didn't own the salon there in 1994, and this is where it was. This is where it was.

I submit to you this, that the commonwealth fed you some crackers, ladies and gentlemen, they fed you some peanuts. When they fed you the crackers and peanut. Then they decided to call Mr. Culbert to the stand, and they poured ink in the water, and then handed it to you and said, here, drink this, its okay, its okay. Culbert is a killer but its okay. You can drink this and no matter if you put sugar in it, if you put honey in it, if you boil it, if you fry it if you throw it out, it's still inky water. You can't get the dirt out, you can't get the corruptness out of that man's mouth, no matter what hand he puts on what Bible. We don't even know his name. How many names did he give us? Let's see. I said why did you give the police so many different names. Well, I gave it to police because I was trying to avoid responsibility. I was trying to avoid apprehension, the same thing he's trying to avoid now. Take a sip. It will quench your thirst. Might kill you, too. Take a sip. That's the man that you have to rely on.

Vernon Daniels, only uttered that he knew Yonzetta Hudson. There was no words from Daniels' that Yonzetta Hudson was involved in anything. You know the only person that got up here, ladies and gentlemen, and told you that Yonzetta Hudson had anything to do with anything was the man that wants you to drink that glass.

Mr. King told you in his opening statement; he said ladies and gentlemen, this case is about money, it's about Yonzetta Hudson having $200,000. Now, ladies and gentlemen, three people said it was two, one person said it was one, and another said it was fifty. But be that as it may, Yonzetta Hudson, we're going to show you evidence that Yonzetta Hudson had money. What evidence from this stand, other than the man that wants you to take a sip, said Yonzetta Hudson had any money in her possession? What evidence did this man put on that stand to indicate that she had any money?

But then it got better. In his opening statement he said, ladies and gentlemen, we will prove that she spent some of the money. What evidence from this stand indicated that she had any money from anyone and spent it? What evidence? But it got better. He said, Ladies and gentlemen, we will prove to you that because she spent the money, she was afraid, so she wanted to hire someone to commit a murder. But it doesn't stop there. It doesn't stop there.

He puts on Mrs. Slade and Mr. Slade has a right to be angry. She lost a son. She has a right to want justice. She lost her son she has the right to be spiteful. It was very tragic, but don't you dare, don't you dare, because of a tragedy commit another one. Don't you dare? Because one thing she said that she didn't say when she was interviewed but she said from the stand for the first time. I answered the telephone. Thank God for sequestration, because then Mr. Slade, who also has the right to be upset, who also has the right to be angry, who also has the right to demand justice, came in here and sat on the stand. I asked him, well, what happened. I didn't even ask him any questions and he said, As a matter of fact, He picked up the phone, and then I heard him, say, all right, a male's name, not Yonzetta Hudson, I'll meet you later. All right. Some male's name, not Yonzetta Hudson's name. I will meet you later.

What's so important about that. First of all, we know now that Mrs. Slade didn't answer the phone but it was her son who picked up the phone. We know that. Her husband is not going to get on here and lie on her. But she did tell you, when I asked the question, that she wants everybody's that's sitting here to pay for her son. No matter what they did or didn't do, they got to pay, because someone said she said something. No that's not justice. Justice is when the right person who committed the crime is punished, not when someone who knows two people from both ends of the spectrum that's involved in sitting here, because she knows 'em. Ladies and gentlemen, I was born in Bedford Stuyvesant in Brooklyn, New York, in a housing project. If you can be convicted for people that you know, I would be under the jail. Doesn't happen in the commonwealth. Didn't happen in New York, and I submit it don't happen in the commonwealth.

But what else from that testimony is important. What else? He said, all right, male name, I will meet you late. Well, that's somewhat different from the theory put forth by the commonwealth where he says this woman paged the man, the man called her back, according to the guy that want you to drink that water right there, and the hit was set up. Mr. King marked carts here in here, ladies and gentlemen, and he showed you a chart of some pager records. Remember that chart? Do you think if that pager had Yonzetta Hudson's number on it, you would have heard about it? Do you think he would have put that evidence on? I submit to you I know the man, he would have.

Michael Slade tells you that his brother had a relationship with another male in the courtroom because they did business with salons. I don't know his reason for not wanting to say that his brother was a drug dealer. It really doesn't matter. But the interesting thing is that, on the 29th of March somebody shot up Randy Slade's car and it was not Yonzetta Hudson, The interesting thing about this is in December, something else happened and it did not involve Yonzetta Hudson, She wasn't a catalyst to anything. But three days later, she's setting up a hit, a contract killing, because its money that no one seems to know where it is. Where is this money, this $600,000? This $200,000 this $100,000 that she set up a hit for? Where is it? Don't you want to know? Then we put special agent Jesse Coleman on the stand, and special agent Coleman, a respected member of the F.B.I. says, that voice you hear is such and such. Well, there's a female voice on here. Oh, that's unknown. Don't you let anyone hoodwink you in this courtroom into believing that is Yonzetta Hudson's voice when we learned it was the voice of Lisa Foxworth. No evidence from this stand proves that the voice on that wiretap is that of Yonzetta Hudson.

Don't you let anyone hoodwink you in this courtroom that that's her voice. No evidence from this stand, none, that that's her voice. The expert, Jesse Coleman, said that female voice is what? Unknown. Don't you let anyone come in this room and try to hoodwink you into thinking that she had something to do with that tape. I don't care what the tape says; it has nothing to do with her.

Well Mr. Shabazz, If you're telling me that the tape has nothing to do with her, that there's no wiretap, the house is totally different from the house this man went to, that the salon was not in existence when he went into the salon, why are we here? Good question. Good question. These photograph's I suspect Mr King will say, well, this was taken in 1999. Sure was. She was arrested and turned herself in in 1998. What the hell I got to take a picture in 1994 for? She's not charged with anything. But ain't nothing changed.

And did you see how Janice Winston got beat up, beat up on the stand? Did you see how Sheila got beat up on the stand? Like, how did you remember this? But you want a murderer, a baby killer who said he went to a place one time; you're supposed to believe him. But when I brought a teacher in here, when I brought someone who's an engineer to testify from that stand that they've been places hundreds of time, you're supposed to believe it? What the hell is this?

Take a sip. No matter what you do, you can't strain or take out the ink once it's in the water. And don't you let anyone hoodwink you into thinking that she chose that witness. Yonzetta Hudson didn't choose anybody. Mr. King can call or not call whoever he wants to. He chose that witness. He made the deal with that witness for 20 to 40 years. He made the deal for the third degree taking away the death penalty.

The young lady is innocent. She's innocent. Not Guilty. Innocent. She had nothing to do with the slaying of Randy Slade. And it hasn't been proven to you in this or any other courtroom in this building. You can't convict anyone on suspicion, supposition. You can't convict someone on association. It has to be evidence. It has to be believable evidence. I was going to speak to you about the benefits as per Mr. Culbert, but I think that's been addressed. He said, hopefully, I'll get out of jail. He said—your recollection controls—I want to do anything I can to assist myself and aid myself in getting out of jail. This man knew that anything he could say doesn't have to be truthful.

The second thing is, what evidence, not argument, what evidence have you heard from that witness stand that puts this woman involved? Ladies and gentlemen Mr. King continued to put on evidence to indicate that the boy had beef with someone and he had a beef with someone in December and March, but then he told you at the same time, flip side, money.

The bottom line is to find her guilty of conspiracy, murder, possession of an instrument of crime, possession of an offensive weapon; you have to rely on the testimony of Stacy Culbert. Quench your thirst. You won't be able to tell anybody else about it, but quench your thirst. Corrupt and polluted source. I don't care if you ran 5K, you ain't drinking that. Don't you drink that, either.

When I sit down my job is going to be done. And I pray to God that I did my job correctly. Mr. King will speak, and then his honor will have the final say as he instructs you on the law. Then your job begins. And as I began with you, I will end with you. I want you to give her the same analytical ability using the same common sense, using the same emotionless, passionless evaluation that you would want if you sat over here and your life was on the line, you give her that same stuff. Thank you

Nas Acquitted November 2, 1999.

Before the verdict is read, Judge James Lineberger cautions those present. His advice is for those who will like the verdict and those who will dislike it. He does not permit outbursts in his courtroom. In fact, all comments should be saved for outside the courtroom. Those who do not heed his caution will be escorted out by sheriff deputies.

The bailiff reads the verdict. Yonzetta Hudson is not guilty on all charges. She says, "Thank God!" Then she turns to Tariq, her attorney, and hugs him so tight around his neck that he tells her she is choking him. She says she doesn't care.

It was a glorious victory over a corrupt criminal justice system, a system that is stacked against you and has all the money in the world to beat you down and keep you down.

After eighteen months in jail and an intense thirty-day trial, Nas is finally acquitted. Her two co-defendants are acquitted also, but they return to prison on other convictions.

Her story is and alternate version of History. Women are the fastest growing population going to jail. According to the bureau of Justice Statistics, 101,179 women were in state or federal prisons by the end of 2003, the first time the number of females behind bars exceeded one hundred thousand. The drug laws and conspiracy laws are largely responsible. The black community has been destroyed by the long-term imprisonment of mothers, usually on conspiracy convictions

Chapter Eighteen

Our Lives After Incarceration

Aginah

Eight years ago I was fighting for my daughter's life and raising Omar, Eric and Aginah E, my three beloved grandchildren. I was deeply depressed. I spent most of my time in bed. After twenty-five years of operating a highly successful hair salon, I closed it down. I did this even though I didn't know how I was going to survive financially or emotionally. A new experience was occurring inwardly.

Today, I know it was the beginning of a renewal of my spiritual growth. I began a journey to inner simplicity. I was experiencing life differently. With life coaching skills I was beginning to clearly see deep subconscious belief patterns that had been dictating the circumstances of my life again and again. For me to change my attitude and mental behavior I had to change counterproductive subconscious beliefs.

I began to see the things I should stop doing, things that created the same unfortunate situations. I could see the dependencies and patterns from which I needed to be free. What was their root? Freedom required that I understand the root of these dependencies and patterns.

The answer was simple. I had wounds that needed healing. I was still in pain from the emotional abuse of previous relationships. I was still in pain from deep emotional trauma from sexual abuse I had experienced as a child at age 4 and then again at age 11 years old. Maybe I will discover other wounds. Healing has begun just by my recognizing my wounds.

The process I describe here has helped me to break down any barriers to achieve my goals that previously seemed unreachable. The things I choose to do I am able to do. I am so thankful.

Nas

Since Nas was acquitted in November 1999, she has switched her career from being a license hair stylist for twenty two years, to begin employment at a city agency with excellent medical and dental benefits and also a 401K. It was one year later that she began preparing to marry. I remember initially holding back, my approval, until several of our friends and clients said that I should support my daughter in this union.

While I was dreading Nas getting married, I planned the wedding ceremony and reception. Nas and her fiancé took care of all the cost associated with their New Year's Eve wedding and reception. I was feeling uneasy about her getting married because the man she was going to legally connect with had already displayed some very disturbing deceptions in their relationship. Plus, I never thought that she truly loved him, anyway. I felt Nas was just trying to prove something to herself. After spending a heartbreaking eighteen months incarcerated, and being home for one year, I thought Nas was searching for someone to love her. For me this marriage was about Nas demonstrating for herself and other people that her fiancée loved her more than she loved him.

She wanted her marriage to be a happy one. I felt Nas was not madly in love with him; it was a matter of pride. Coming out of eighteen months of incarceration, I felt Nas wanted the attention of a man. It's easy for me to see how she would want her husband to be her property. That's what she was during her incarceration—The State's Property. Nas didn't want him involved with anyone else, so in order to achieve this, if it meant a marriage, she was willing to take that risk. Five years ago, I would listen to Nas speak about him and would hear strong emotions in her voice. I could see her getting frustrated in her physical appearance trying to defend his behavior.

Nas bought two wedding dresses. A Vera Wang dress that she purchased was too small, by the time she sent out her wedding invitations. She had to purchase another dress, which had to be altered after she gave birth on September 4, 2000 to Anisaa, an adorable baby girl. Anisaa came to us three months before the wedding. Nas has two daughters. Her first daughter Aginah E is now eighteen and Anisaa is five.

Before the wedding, her fiancée purchased a matching set of beautiful white gold wedding rings—a diamond band and one-and-a-half-carat solitaire diamond.

Nas was an exquisite bride. The cream-colored satin dress with its soft delicate lace framing her light bronze complexion was a beautiful image, one I have not forgotten. Her full bouquet of peach and cream roses completed the perfect picture.

The wedding ceremony was held in the northeast section of Philadelphia at a place called Arthur's Caterers. Nas' older son Omar gave her away. Yvonne, her loyal client and someone she admired, was her matron of honor. She had two bridesmaids Deidra, who was her childhood friend, and Shannon, who was a stylist at the salon and one of her best friends.

A reception for one hundred of close family and friends immediately followed the ceremony. Guest were lavishly treated to delicious hors d'oeuvres, chicken and fish dinner. Most of the guest took home a generous slice of the three tiered wedding cake. It was New Years Eve, December 31, 2000.

The marriage failed six months later. There were many compelling reasons why the marriage failed. Yet, the most basic was that he was not meeting the family's basic needs such as the rent, gas, electric and food. From the very beginning, my opinion of her husband was that he didn't deserve her, but then again, she had to find this out for herself. Mister (like the man in color purple) was very deceptive!

Nas will have difficulties to face now that she is out of jail, being the mother of four beautiful children ages five, eighteen, twenty and twenty two. Her oldest three have graduated from high school. She is also faced with resisting the lure of easy money and the material things that can be gained from dating men with questionable characters. My son, Sultan was adamant when he said, "He would bet his life on the fact that his sister will never take that route again, ever in life. I have faith that Nas has learned to be more careful regarding the company she keeps."

She has been working with the city agency for five years, appreciating and enjoying living an uncomplicated life in a small house located in a suburban community with her four children Omar, Eric, Aginah E, and Anisaa. The three older children are overjoyed to have their mother back. She also enjoys her new lifestyle with new friends who are her co-workers.

Simply making the choice to be in the company of men with questionable character can be dangerous to one's life both in terms of being caught in the cross fire, guilty by association for just being with them and benefiting financially from their illegal enterprises. And don't forget to include the professional men who are abusive both verbally and physically. It all leads to the same place.

Afterword

Writing this book has been a cleansing experience for me. I was able to revisit and face painful memories. I have walked away from those memories, now looking back at them as experiences. I am not the same. I love the woman I am today. I am not married. But my friends say I am married to the Internet. You can find me at my computer day and night. It serves as company and of course, as a source of information and knowledge about many different things.

I thank God for giving me the understanding and the discipline to have peace from the inside out. I own a small salon, one to which I can walk and at which I serve a small number of people who have been loyal clients over the years. I pray. I meditate. I take herbs and natural supplements to support my health, which is basically good. I am back to exercising. And I manage my time.

I also manage my money even though it is quite a bit less than I am accustomed to having. I no longer frequent the upscale designer clothing stores. I don't drive a Mercedes or a seven-series BMW. And I would not think of doing so without such luxury being backed up with a mutual fund, a retirement fund, and at least several healthy bank accounts.

Effect and Cures

The problems such as the ones many of us have experienced don't happen all of a sudden. They begin slowly and grow. A young woman might be attracted to the big-talking guy—he's cool in her young eyes. If she is successful at capturing his attention, she gains a sense of power because of who he is portrayed to be in certain circles of influence.

This is true, especially for women who don't know who they really are inside. They seek and define themselves in the personality of a man. Women gain a sense of power and self-esteem by capturing a man's attention. This can be a seed of codependence—a woman who is more childlike emotionally, who needs to find her significance in the personality of a man. When women do that, they open themselves up to all kinds of unscrupulous characters because they are not looking for a good man; they are seeking a man that looks good. Lots of women fall into the clutches of a real psychopath because he could play the part and look the part.

The cure has some long roots to be cut off; you must dig deep. Dig deep? Yes, inside to search for yourself. In that process, you destroy the roots. When they die, nail the coffin shut.

It's May 2001; I lay totally relaxed on a beach in Nassau, Bahamas, reflecting on my life's' journey. While being warmed by the sun and cooled down with a dip in the ocean, I am listening to the roar and revisiting the lives of four generations, my maternal grandmother, my mother, my life and my daughter's life. What stands out most is that the choices we've all made are similar.

By making the decision to tell my story to the public, I put myself in the way of insulting comments about my character. By stripping away my modesty and revealing myself as a complicated person who is not perfect, I am allowing others to see for themselves that a less-than-perfect human being like me can help others by speaking out about my faults and the poor choices I made.

Sistah friends, I brought to you my life experiences because some women need to know they're not alone and bringing to you *CHOICEZ* tells the story—even I was afraid to write, but I did. *CHOICEZ* has helped me on my healing journey. I've learned the lessons and moved on—so can you. Please take the time to think it through, whatever it may be. Take heed to God's warning signs, pray, meditate, read, talk to someone, and ponder your decisions. Right now, make the decision to "make the right choice." They impact our lives.

A Word About Money

While some of the numbers I give below may not be applicable today, the basic advice leads to learning the road to financial harmony.

I experienced so much financial disharmony that I couldn't leave it out of this book. You hear on every other television program people educating you about financial planning, financial growth. "If it were so easy, then why isn't everyone doing it?" I asked. Lack of knowledge. Our schools don't teach money skills, our parents don't teach about money. But today take heed—there are many people to turn to and books to read. If you only would pay attention now and take full responsibility for your own future, even if you think you do everything else badly, I guarantee you that someday you'll be rich. "Can one start today?" I ask. Yes, let's get started. Go to a trustworthy and reliable person, who knows a lot about money, or a banking institution and tell them what you want to achieve. "Is it possible?" you may ask. I read a book many years ago called *The Richest Man in Babylon*. It taught me that wealth is beyond your wildest dreams and is possible if you follow the golden rule: saving ten percent of your income. I followed that rule many times and eventually squandered the money on material things or helping others. Saving money is not easy especially when your wants become your needs. Did I need a new car every two to three years or did I just want one?

Investing ten to fifteen percent of all you make for a long term goal. If you invest two hundred dollars a month for twelve months for the next ten years, how much money do you think you'll end up with? Then add the compounded interest and multiply that by additional ten to fifteen percent savings monthly. Are you impressed to have saved that amount of money?

Things are going to get more expensive. Mortgages are going to continue to rise in price and Range Rovers are going to cost more. So if you start now saving ten percent, you'll be parking your convertible BMW beside your vacation home in the Bahamas. Your salaries will also rise and your ten percent savings will grow. I have to ask myself, given another opportunity to save, is it going to work for me now in my fifty-seventh year? Of course it is, if I pay myself first. You can arrange for ten to twenty percent of your income to go directly into a separate bank account at a different bank other than your Primary one, and from there to an investment plan. This makes it easy because you don't even see it.

Sister friends, it's so easy for us to become distracted with the here and now and to get wrapped up in living for today but we sell ourselves short when we don't prepare for the larger investments we want. Now I'm not talking about a Mercedes Benz or your first apartment. I'm talking about the House you want to own one day. I'm talking about how you plan to pay for your child's education—are your debts structured properly? I'm talking about a life insurance policy so if you were to leave this earth today or tomorrow you don't leave any financial burdens to your family—is your will up-to-date? Some of us can't go on a vacation until our next check comes because we don't know what it means to invest. That word sounds scary. But it takes homework to know what these things mean.

In an *Essence* article, The CEO and chairperson of BET networks stated that "many influences are common to all women, but Black women, in particular, have often been the heart of the family. They have had to support their loved ones and often not having enough money. As a result and because of the perceived risk involved in investing, they want to hold on to that cash-keep it in the bank or hide it under the mattress-as opposed to thinking about how to invest it." I think the time was way past due for us to let go of that fear and grasp our financial security by the bullhorns and stop waiting for that lottery to hit because it may never come. Some of us would have rather taken $50 to play the lottery but did not want to save it. At some point, you will still be looking for instant gratification.

After reading the article I thought to myself: "SISTAHGIRL, GET YOUR MONEY STRAIGHT!"

Made in the USA
Monee, IL
04 November 2026

67378325R00098